JAN. 1996

CHINESE AMERICANS

By Tina Moy

Marshall Cavendish
New York • London • Toronto

Published by
Marshall Cavendish Corporation
2415 Jerusalem Avenue
P.O. Box 587
North Bellmore, New York 11710, U.S.A.

© Marshall Cavendish Corporation, 1995

Edited, designed, and produced by Water Buffalo Books, Milwaukee

Editor and contributing writer: Susan Rensberger

Project director: Mark Sachner
Art director: Sabine Beaupré
Picture researcher: Diane Laska
Editorial: Eileen Foran
Cover Design: Lee Goldstein
Marshall Cavendish development editor: MaryLee Knowlton
Marshall Cavendish editorial director: Evelyn Fazio

Picture Credits: © Archive Photos/American Stock: 20; © Archive Photos/Thornton: 28; Sabine Beaupré 1994: 7, 19; © The Bettmann Archive: 6, 12 (top), 21, 22, 25, 26, 27, 29, 47; © T. DeLamo/H. Armstrong Roberts: 41; © Gemignani/H. Armstrong Roberts: 11; Courtesy of Gerald (Kwok Jung) and Hannah Chow (Sook Jung) Moy: 17; © Photosearch/Nick Patrinos: 1, 4, 37, 51; © Reuters/Bettmann: 9, 12 (bottom), 14, 16, 65, 67, 71, 72 (top), 75; © Springer/Bettmann Film Archive: 68; © Katrina Thomas: Cover, 18, 30, 31, 32, 36, 38, 39, 42, 43, 44, 46, 50, 53, 54, 57, 60, 62, 63, 64, 73, 74; © UPI/Bettmann: 13, 66, 69, 72 (bottom); Courtesy of Anna Moy Wong and Walter Wong: 58, 59

Library of Congress Cataloging-in-Publication Data

Moy, Tina.
    Chinese Americans / Tina Moy.
       p.   cm. — (Cultures of America)
    Includes bibliographical references and index.
    ISBN 1-85435-780-8 (set). — ISBN 1-85435-785-9 : $19.95
    1. Chinese Americans—Juvenile literature. I. Title. II. Series.
    E184.C5M69   1995
    305.895'1—dc20   94-12601
                                                         CIP
                                                          AC

To PS – MS
For Por Por and Gong Gong (Moy and Chow), especially Mom and Dad – TM

Printed and bound in the U.S.A.

CONTENTS

INTRODUCTION

They hold the world record. With the longest continuous history of any civilization, the Chinese have an impressive list of contributions to world cultures. Things we take for granted today — paper, kites, pasta, fortune cookies with your Chinese takeout food, and July 4th fireworks — were brought to the West and America by the Chinese. Drawing from a rich ancestral heritage and traditions that date back thousands of years, Chinese Americans have been sharing their innovative and tasteful cooking techniques and recipes, their gracious style and hospitality, and their wonderfully bright and noisy celebrations with the rest of the U.S. since the nineteenth century.

Chinese Americans are a strong and bright thread stitched in the American tapestry, bringing to mainstream culture a long tradition of ingenuity, commitment, and integrity. Their threads have been tattered, along with those woven by other non-European immigrants, and they have been treated like foreigners in a land they helped build along with immigrants from all over the world. In spite of exhibiting undying hope and enthusiasm, their contributions were not always acknowledged.

Early Chinese immigrants were unfortunate targets of discrimination based on others' fear of job loss, economic insecurity, and the unknown. Anti-immigration laws kept Chinese and other Asians from immigrating to America for more than half a century. Rather than giving up, pioneering Chinese who came to America in the early nineteenth century dug in their heels and worked ten times harder than fellow railroad workers, gold miners, and farmers. Today, Chinese Americans make their way in all walks of life.

With China and other Asian countries looking increasingly attractive in the global marketplace, Chinese Americans are proudly wearing their individual coat of success, crafted with the art of patience, ingenuity, and tradition. With it, they continue to overcome the cold reality of discrimination to enrich their own and others' lives. Chinese Americans are venturing beyond the American Dream of their early immigrant relatives, still holding onto the best of traditional Chinese values and culture.

This Sung Dynasty artwork shows women adorned in silk, a fabric that Western traders found valuable. China became a desirable trading destination because of its rich culture and civilization.

LEAVING A HOMELAND
CHINA FROM ANCIENT TIMES

Long before this nation was founded or the Americas were invaded by adventurers from across the seas; before kings battled in Europe, or Rome ruled the Mediterranean world; before the birth of Christ in the Middle East or the building of the pyramids in Egypt, there was China.

As early as 5000 B.C., archaeologists estimate, people living in what is today the People's Republic of China grew rice and millet and wove silk. Early forms of Chinese writing have been found on bones dating from 1300 B.C., some one thousand years before the Trojan War of the ancient Greek empire.

Throughout the centuries, the Chinese created paper and printing, gunpowder, magnetic compasses, crossbows and stirrups useful in battle, cast iron for tools and bridges, nails and armor, and religious statues. Many of these inventions reached the Middle East and Europe or were discovered independently by the Western world, centuries after the Chinese had begun using them. Yet their use changed the rest of the world more than it changed China.

Poverty, the decline of the Chinese empire, and work opportunities abroad led to a huge exodus out of southeastern China in the late 1800s.

The World's Oldest Living Civilization

With the world's longest continuous civilization, China was for centuries one of the most advanced societies on earth. When European traders first began arriving in China in the sixteenth century, the Chinese were self-sufficient and had little need for anything from the West.

Yet China was a very traditional society, built on the principals of Confucius (a name used by seventeenth-century Western missionaries for the early Chinese philosopher Kong

CHINESE WRITING AND PRONUNCIATION

Chinese writing is ideographic — that is, based on the idea a word conveys rather than its sound. Each Chinese character represents an entire word and tells the reader nothing about how that word sounds when spoken. People from different parts of China can read the same written words but speak them so differently that they cannot understand each other. The Chinese language includes about fifty thousand characters, each as different as the letters of our alphabet, though it's only necessary to memorize three or four thousand for everyday communication.

Western languages, on the other hand, including English, are phonetic. The twenty-six letters in our alphabet represent sounds, and so the same alphabet can be used to spell many words and even several languages, such as French, German, Spanish, or Italian. Knowing the sound represented by each letter, a person who doesn't know the meaning of a word can nevertheless figure out its pronunciation. This isn't true of Chinese.

When Europeans encountered Chinese language, they wanted to write it down in a form they could read. This meant using the Roman, or Latin, alphabet used for European languages to represent the sounds of spoken Chinese. This was very difficult, especially since the Chinese use combinations of rising, falling, and level tones to change the meaning of words. Early attempts to Romanize Chinese failed to capture accurately many Chinese pronunciations.

The system used by most Westerners today to spell Chinese words is called *pinyin,* the same system used in mainland China. Letters have the same sound in pinyin as they do in English, with a few exceptions, for example:

c sounds like "ts" as in "tsetse fly."
q sounds like "ch" as in "chair."
x sounds like "sh" as in "shirt."
zh sounds like "j" as in "jet."

Thus the country named for its first emperor, Qin Shihuangdi, is pronounced "China," not "Quina."

Qiu, because the Westerners couldn't pronounce his Chinese title "Kong Fuzi," meaning "Master Kong"). Confucius, who lived about 551-479 B.C., taught that obedience to authority and respect for elders was what held society together. These values made Chinese society orderly, but they also made change difficult. Peasants tended to stay poor, partly because land was scarce and partly because they were taught to submit to fate and those placed above them in society.

As Western cultures developed new technologies over the last few centuries and began a process of rapid change, China held to its traditional agricultural economy until the latter half of the twentieth century, when the Communist government tried to rapidly industrialize the country. The greed of foreign powers in the nineteenth and twentieth centuries drained the wealth of China while refusing to submit to Chinese control of either trade or foreign settlers in China. This outside influence, combined with traditional Chinese resistance to change, gradually transformed China into a nation that became, despite its stable culture and family structure, one of the poorest on earth, at least by Western standards.

Chinese farmers outside Beijing spread fertilizer with shovels. Even in the twentieth century, change is slow in coming to the country's traditional agricultural economy.

Power Lay in Family Position

Throughout its history, family has been extremely important to the people of China. For example, Chinese history is divided into periods called dynasties, which are named for the family that ruled during that time. Also, Chinese names place the family name before the individual's name, emphasizing the importance of family. Thus Cynthia Jones would be Jones Cynthia if her name were Chinese, and Chiang Kai-shek would be called Mr. Chiang in the United States.

Loyalty of children to parents was considered one's highest duty in life in historic China, and an important function of the family was to care for elderly parents and worship their spirits after they died. Sons were valued much more than daughters because they were expected to live with their parents and support them in their old age. If a family had enough wealth, all of its sons would continue to live with their parents and farm the family land or work in the family business after they married, raising their own children in the same household. In a poorer family, only the oldest son would play this role, while younger sons had to find other ways to support themselves, their wives, and their children.

Daughters, by contrast, were expected to live with their parents only until they were old enough to marry. Some were married

9

very young, at twelve or thirteen, to men chosen by their parents. A woman was expected to spend the rest of her life as a member of her husband's family, working in the household run by her mother-in-law and worshipping her husband's ancestors. Because she did not contribute to supporting her own parents or worship them after their death, a daughter was considered more a burden than a benefit to a family. Sometimes poor families drowned baby girls rather than spend money raising them, only to see them join another family. Today, the Chinese government prohibits killing infants. Yet because government policy also pressures parents to have only one child, journalists report that the tradition of secretly killing girl babies in order to raise a son continues in some parts of China, and up to a million little girls have disappeared.

Law, Order, and Punishment

The larger society mirrored the family hierarchy, though in some respects the family remained the strongest authority. Families were expected to control the actions of their members, and Chinese society relied less on courts of law than on fathers and grandfathers to maintain social order.

To help make sure that families did their jobs, Chinese law held family members responsible for each other, while the father could be punished for the wrongdoing of anyone else in the family. Punishments for violence, or even speaking harshly, against a family member were severe and defined by law. Striking an elder could be punished by death.

Similarly, the local official chosen to oversee a district was held responsible for crimes committed by anyone in that district. Punishments were cruel and rigidly defined by

FASHION TAKEN TO EXTREMES

One of the most visible and widely known signs of the subjugation of women in Chinese culture was the custom of footbinding. Starting with a fad among those in the royal court in the tenth century, the custom of footbinding spread through other levels of society. Based on male ideas that small feet made women more attractive, footbinding was designed to make girls marriageable by keeping their feet from becoming more than three inches long. To prevent the feet from growing, they were kept tightly wrapped in strips of fabric, day and night for as long as ten years.

Around age five to eight, a girl's foot would be bent down and bound into position with the smaller toes turned under. But the girl's feet would not stop growing. The arches gradually broke and her foot grew into a grotesque shape. She would be in

constant pain, never able to run again, walking only on her heels. Even standing would become difficult. Only after her feet had stopped growing in her teen years would the pain subside, but she would remain disabled for life. Even though footbinding was practiced by some peasants, it was most common among the wealthier classes.

While footbinding was an extreme example, many cultures have standards for attractiveness that not only restrict women's freedom of movement but sometimes even mutilate their bodies. Skirts, corsets, and high heels are all examples of restrictive fashions that women wore while men dressed in pants and flat shoes. Even in our society today, a woman dressing up for an important meeting or an evening out will most often choose clothes not for comfort but because they meet social expectations.

Girls at a ceremony in Nanning. Conditions for girls in China have improved from earlier days.

law, favoring slow or gruesome deaths. For example, highway robbery was punished by crucifixion or decapitation. A grave robber was placed in a wooden crate with only his head sticking out and left to starve or die of heatstroke. Treason could be punished by the slow dismemberment of the body, and by beheading all male family members of the traitor. Torture was used to extract confessions and even to elicit evidence from witnesses at trial.

Such a brutal legal system gave rise to the Chinese saying, "In death avoid hell; in life avoid courts of law." Offsetting the cruelty of the prescribed punishments was the fact that a few policemen were in charge of large areas, increasing the chance that an offense would not come to light. Nevertheless, those officials who were in charge of enforcing the law had almost total power over anyone charged

with a crime, and even the threat of being brought to court could result in enough bribes to make the official wealthy.

The Reluctant Soil

Though China is the largest country in the world, a subcontinent extending from as far north as Canada to as far south as Cuba, only about one-third of that land is livable and only 15 percent can be farmed. Because western China is so mountainous, most people live in eastern China. While Chinese cities are among the most crowded in the world, most people still live as they have for centuries in country villages, farming small plots of land by hand to feed their families.

Hunger has always been a problem in China. In the past, land was owned by landlords but farmed by peasants who had to give much of their crops to the landlord as rent. In a year of drought or flood, the peasant family might have nothing left to eat once the landlord was paid. Even today, with so little land for farming and so many people to feed, hunger is a constant threat. There is no room for raising large animals like cattle and horses that need pasture and eat grain that humans could eat themselves. Farmers keep small animals like pigs, chickens, and ducks to supplement their diet of grains, vegetables, and fruit.

Northeastern China, where the country's earliest civilization developed, has very cold winters and hot summers with uneven rainfall. The summer winds that blow from the South China Sea drop most of their rain on southern China, leaving little for the north. Drought and famine are common, and over the centuries millions have died of starvation. On the other hand, the rains that do come sometimes cause floods that destroy homes and crops, resulting in more starvation.

An elderly man eats a bowl of rice along a city street in China. Rice has long been the main staple in the diets of many Chinese people.

A farmer weighs a watermelon for sale at his street stall in Daxing, China's self-styled watermelon capital. Daxing is in northern China, where fruit, vegetables, and wheat grow well.

Peasant rice farmers squat in rice paddies to plant the spring crop in tropical southeastern China.

Northern people often live as their ancestors did, in villages ringed by earthen walls. Village houses are made of mud bricks and even today may have paper instead of glass for windows. In some places, cave homes are carved, as they have been for twelve thousand years, into hills of the compact yellow soil, called loess, that makes up the region. Northern farmers raise wheat and millet, grains that grow well in dry areas, as well as fruit and vegetables.

Southeastern China is the tropical land of rice paddies worked by water buffalo and farmers in the conical straw hats Westerners often picture when they think of China. Rice has always been the main crop of the south, because there rainfall is plentiful and the weather so warm that two or even three crops could be grown in a year. Traditional houses of the south were often built of bamboo, and

many still are. People also live in small apartments in crowded cities, or on small houseboats that float on the many rivers and lakes, and in coastal ports.

Just as in the north, land in the south is precious and every inch possible is used for food production. Flat lowlands are devoted to raising rice, the most important food crop in China.

Over the centuries, farmers learned to raise crops even on steep hillsides by creating terraces — flat, step-like fields carved into the sloping hills. There they grow fruit and vegetables, as well as tea, cotton, and mulberry trees, whose leaves are fed to silk worms. The cocoons spun by these worms are the source of silk fibers, one of the products that Europeans were most interested in buying from the Chinese when they came seeking trade in the sixteenth century.

Thousands of people rally along the Great Wall, which stretches across northern China. China is a vast land of mountains, plateaus, and coastal plains where more than one billion people live.

A World Apart

With so many resources and such a highly developed culture, historic China had little reason for contact with other nations. There was little reason for the Chinese to risk leaving their homes for other lands, because the population had not yet outgrown the land's ability to feed its people.

At the same time, few outsiders reached China. Deserts and mountain ranges on the west, north, and south, and oceans on the east, made the Chinese empire hard to reach from the outside.

Though occasionally peoples from the north attacked and ruled China, eventually these foreign-led dynasties adopted Chinese culture and customs. Not until the nineteenth century, when Western nations used their more advanced weapons and stronger military to force changes upon China, did foreign contact threaten Chinese civilization.

The West Breaks Through

When European explorers arrived, led by the Portuguese in 1516, they came looking for exotic goods they could sell in Europe. From the Chinese point of view, the vast empire of China was the center of the world, with its long history, wealth, and sophisticated systems of government, industry, and arts. Chinese emperors were willing to permit just enough contact with "barbaric" European traders to sell some of China's goods — tea, silk, and porcelain particularly.

Because the Chinese refused to trade, Europeans had to pay cash for the goods they purchased. English traders discovered they could raise the money by bringing opium from the British colony of India, where it was produced and sold legally, and smuggling it into China, where it was illegal. By 1839, the British were making more than $18 million a year selling opium to a market of perhaps two to four million addicted Chinese.

When the British government refused to help stop the destructive flow of opium into China, the Chinese finally seized all the opium from the British traders and dumped it into the sea. The British fought back in what came to be known as the Opium War of 1839.

The British easily won, and the peace treaties they imposed on the Chinese gave foreigners more rights and powers in China than ever before. For the Chinese, it was the beginning of the end of their proud and independent empire, a process that would make the already harsh conditions of life for most Chinese increasingly unbearable.

Western Influence: Power and Opportunity

After the Opium War, the Chinese were forced to turn over Hong Kong to the British, open more ports to foreign trade, and let foreigners rule those cities. Chinese living under foreign rule had no rights in their own land. Foreign missionaries were allowed throughout China for the first time, spreading Western ideas about religion and culture that were in conflict with Chinese traditions.

European visitors sometimes published long accounts of their travels in China, which remained unknown and therefore exotic to most Europeans. One such traveler, a French writer named M. Huc, who published a two-volume report titled *The Chinese Empire* in 1855, described the backbreaking work of Chinese farmers. Because land was divided among sons, he said, it was almost always farmed in small plots, especially in the south. Even on larger farms occasionally found in the north, only simple tools were used. He gave this account of plowing:

In the south, the rice-fields are usually tilled with buffaloes, called "aquatic oxen." In the north, our common domestic oxen are made use of, as well as horses, mules, and asses; and more than once it happened to us to see a plough drawn by a woman, while her husband walked be-

OPIUM: A CURSE IMPOSED ON CHINA

Opium is an addictive drug made from the opium poppy. The Chinese had grown and used opium for medicinal purposes — relieving pain, stopping spasms, calming sickness — long before it became widely used as a recreational drug in the seventeenth century.

But opium and the medications made from it, including morphine, heroin, and codeine, are habit forming. Once the practice of smoking opium spread — due in large part to the trafficking of the drug in China by British smugglers looking for a market to exploit — drug use had much the same effects on nineteenth-century Chinese society that we see from drug use in Western societies today.

Opium destroyed individual lives and families. The need to do anything in order to obtain the drug drove addicts to commit violent crimes. The high price of opium corrupted officials who were bribed by smugglers to allow the traffic to continue. No one knew how to stop the demand or supply of the drug. And behind its import were a foreign government, individual importers, and corrupt officials all willing to sacrifice lives for profit.

China's Yangtze River, the world's fourth-longest river, offers vistas that have awed visitors for centuries. One is the Three Gorges section shown here. Many rivers flow into the Yangtze, draining about one-fifth of China's waters.

hind, and guided it. Pitiable it is to see the poor things sticking their little [bound] feet into the ground as they go, and drawing them painfully out again, and so hopping from one end of the furrow to the other.

As Europeans were discovering life in China, so Chinese peasants were starting to learn about Western life. Westerners brought with them a standard of living that was unfamiliar to most Chinese. Most Chinese lived a life of hard labor, like the woman pulling the plow or the men who carried people in rickshas, the Chinese alternative to carriages.

As Chinese peasants faced increased hardship at home with little opportunity for a better life, emigrating became a dream worth pursuing, if only for the purpose of bringing back wealth to their families; few intended to leave their homeland permanently. Defeat after devastating defeat by European nations and Japan had weakened the power of the Chinese emperor. Taxes were high, rents were high, famine and flood were widespread and making peasant life miserable. Repeated rebellions by peasants trying to get land for themselves and take back control of China from foreigners killed millions of Chinese.

As the government failed to either improve the lives of its people or protect them from invasion and control by foreigners, another rebellion arose in 1900 to kill foreigners and Christian Chinese. Foreign nations sent a powerful military force to put down the rebellion. The nation was again humiliated, and in 1912 the last emperor abdicated, ending the era of dynasties and throwing traditional Chinese society into chaos. For some, it was a good time to look for a better life elsewhere, and until the United States passed laws prohibiting their entrance from the late 1800s until the 1940s, many Chinese left home for America and elsewhere.

COMING TO AMERICA: A LOVE STORY

Gerald caught his first glimpse of Hannah when he saw her picture in a friend's album. When he asked his friend who the pretty woman was, she told him that Hannah was one of her best friends from school in Hong Kong. He didn't know it then, but this was the young woman he would fall in love with and marry.

The year was 1955. Gerald had come to America from China in 1951 at sixteen to live and work with his dad. America's Chinese Exclusion Act (finally repealed in 1943) prevented Gerald's mother from joining his father, who had left China before Gerald was born. Like many immigrants, Gerald's dad worked long hours to save enough money to send his family until they could be reunited.

Gerald missed his mom and wrote to her often. She urged him to find a nice girl from China and settle down. A kind, good-looking person, he had no trouble making friends with the women in his new home, but none of them made him think of marriage. Now twenty-one, he returned to visit China, planning to carry out his mom's hopes. Arriving in Guangdong in 1956 after a five-year absence, he set out to see his mother again — and to meet the woman whose photo had caught his eye.

Gerald visited his friend's family in Hong Kong, bringing them the gifts she had bought them in America. And then he met Hannah. He instantly knew he was in love with her, and he set about trying to get to know her. But their paths would not cross again for three months. Meanwhile, Gerald dated other young women, one of them a pen pal of two years. Many of them showed an interest in Gerald, but he could think only of Hannah. He repeatedly asked her to go out with him, only to have her brothers warn her against him. After all, they told her, they had seen him out every night with a different woman! Feeling discouraged, Gerald decided it would be better to stay single.

With his visa due to expire, Gerald left his apartment to make plans to go back to America. He was halfway down the block when a neighbor shouted for him to come back. A beautiful woman was ringing his doorbell. He returned to find that his housekeeper had let someone named Hannah stroll into his apartment.

Gerald extended his visa for three months. This time, he dated only Hannah. After many dinners, movies, and gifts, Gerald asked Hannah the biggest two-part question of their lives: "If you want to go to America, would you like to marry me?" Without hesitation, she said yes. They honeymooned in Hong Kong for a month before Gerald had to go back to America. Hannah would join him there later, after her immigration records were approved.

Hannah could only imagine what her new home would be like. But four months later, with love in her heart, tears in her eyes, and visions of America playing in her head like a Hollywood movie, Hannah bid farewell to family and friends. She would soon join her husband in America.

A grandmother and her grandson enjoy spending time together in a neighborhood in New York City's Chinatown. This was rare in the nineteenth and early twentieth centuries, when most Chinese immigrants were men separated from their families when they came to America.

CHAPTER TWO

LIFE IN A NEW LAND
FROM VISIONS OF GOLD TO CULTURE SHOCK

The British victory in the Opium War (1839-1842) marked the beginning of a long decline for China under the Qing (pronounced "Ching") Dynasty. Still largely a society of rural peasants dependent on farming, the country was stricken with mass famines, floods, peasant revolts, and increasingly corrupt public officials.

Given these conditions, the Chinese began looking outside their homeland for hope and a better life. Many Chinese families sent their sons and husbands to China's coastal cities to find work. There the men signed up to work as unskilled laborers and often were sent abroad to such places as Peru, Cuba, Mexico, Southeast Asia, Canada, Hawaii, and California.

Though leaving their country was forbidden by warlords who ruled areas of China, many daring Chinese, especially from the Guangdong Province, saved as much money as they could to buy transportation abroad. Workers who could not afford the full price of a ticket signed labor contracts that allowed

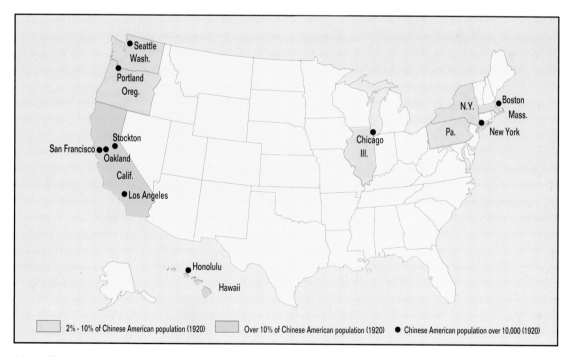

2% - 10% of Chinese American population (1920)   Over 10% of Chinese American population (1920)   ● Chinese American population over 10,000 (1920)

Most Chinese immigrants first came to Hawaii or settled on the West Coast of the United States, later migrating east to settle throughout the country.

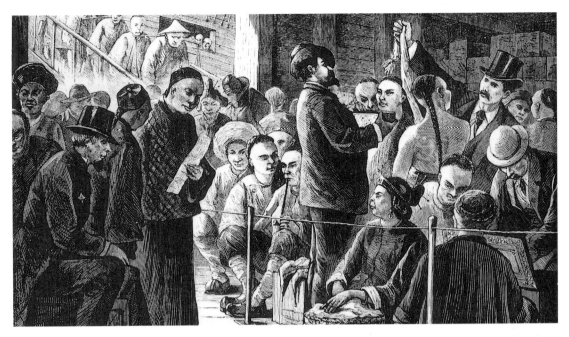

Early immigrants arrive in the late 1870s at the "Golden Mountain," San Francisco, where their first encounter with America is likely to be at a detention area. Many felt frightened and isolated as they were inspected and interrogated before being allowed into the country.

them to pay for their passage out of future earnings. Most didn't realize that these contracts could make them indentured servants. The contracts obligated them to work for the person who paid their passage, usually at very low wages set by the employer, until the debt was repaid.

The Golden Mountain

Thousands of Chinese emigrants stowed aboard old ships for a grueling four-month ocean journey to M*aiguo* (pronounced "may gwau"). *Maiguo,* the name given to America, is Chinese for the "beautiful country." Leaving their families behind was a very hard decision for Chinese men to make, given the Chinese belief in family togetherness and loyalty. Yet this same loyalty and sense of duty to family drove them to travel thousands of miles by ship to San Francisco. Most hoped to work for just a few years in the United States and then return home with their new-found wealth. Their hearts were with their families back in China.

In 1848, the discovery of gold in California set off another large exodus from China. Stories of riches in America led to the Chinese name for California, *Gam San,* which means "Golden Mountain." Because China's Guangdong Province and its port city, Guangdong (Canton), were the major point of American contact with China, it was from here that most of the nineteenth-century immigrants left for America.

Imagine their fear and disappointment when they finally reached American shores with visions of gold, only to be given an unfriendly reception by the "white barbarians" (as some Chinese called Americans of European descent) who awaited their arrival. U.S. officials set up several categories of immigrants allowed to enter the country, and during the period of the Chinese Exclusion Act, Chinese faced obstacles beyond those encountered by European immigrants. From 1882, the year the Exclusion Act went into effect, until 1910, Chinese immigrants were held for questioning and processing at a wharf shed on the San Francisco waterfront.

Between 1910 and 1940, many Chinese immigrants were detained in San Francisco Bay at Angel Island, where they were interrogated for a few hours, physically inspected for contagious diseases, and often kept for months and even years before being allowed to go on to the California mainland. Hundreds of Chinese died while awaiting entry under inhumane conditions at this detention center. They were housed in large rooms crowded with double- and triple-bunk beds and treated as if they were prisoners behind the high fences surrounding the dormitories and tiny recreation yards. Dark paper covered the windows of their rooms, blocking their view of San Francisco, just as the entire ordeal had blocked, seemingly forever, their journey to the Golden Mountain.

The Chinese had already endured feeling like foreigners in their own homeland, where the British and other Europeans had taken increasing control of the country since the Opium War. Now they faced hostility and prejudice from those of European descent who had already settled in the U.S. and didn't welcome the Chinese here, either. While many recent arrivals had to endure name calling and other humiliations, the Chinese were singled out for special abuse because of their outward appearance, which was "different" from that of the European American

Anti-Chinese sentiment grew, spurred on and demonstrated by cartoons like this from the 1870s showing mobs lynching Chinese workers.

majority. Cartoons exaggerated their Asian characteristics and pictured them as animal-like, making fun of the different clothes and hairstyles they brought from China.

"Foreign" Fashions and Beliefs

In addition to their appearance and language, which seemed more "foreign" than most European tongues, the Chinese also brought to America new tastes in food and art, as well as social customs, manners, and beliefs, that were different from those of most European cultures.

Oriental goods imported from China during the 1800s, including Chinese-styled furniture, silks, and paintings, were popular

Early Chinese immigrants came with such traditional styles as the nankeen suits, silk hats, cloth slippers, and long pigtails (called queues) modeled by these men.

China, was not as suitable for the colder and damper weather in northern California. They also found that the rough terrain of the gold fields required tougher shoes and boots than they needed in the farm fields of Guangdong.

Hairstyles set the Chinese apart, too. When living in China, most men under the Qing Dynasty were required to wear their waist-long black hair in a pigtail known as a queue (pronounced "kew") to show their loyalty to their Manchurian rulers. Many Chinese men kept their queues after they arrived in America to make sure they would be accepted back into their homeland when they returned to their families. This was one more style other immigrant groups couldn't understand, not having this kind of rule in their own native countries.

In contrast to the overwhelming influence of Christianity in the religious lives of most European Americans, the Chinese have a long history of blending different religions. One longstanding belief is reincarnation, the idea that after death people return to live another life on earth. Christian missionaries attempted to convert the Chinese by setting up schools and churches in China. But Christianity was quite new to the Chinese at that time, and most Chinese still held beliefs from their own traditional and ancient religions, Buddhism, Confucianism, and Taoism. Because the Chinese tolerated new religions themselves, including the Christianity introduced by Westerners into China, they did not expect a negative reaction in America to their practice of worshipping their ancestors by burning incense at temple altars.

in America, where the culture they represented seemed exotic. It is all the more ironic that when people from that land rich with natural and manmade resources made their way to America, they found themselves unwanted and ridiculed for their foreign style of dress and their customs.

Newly arrived Chinese immigrants wore traditional blue nankeen blouses, baggy trousers, cloth slippers, and wide straw hats. They soon learned that their clothing, perfect for the semitropical climate they left in southern

This basic lack of understanding between different cultures prevented the different immigrant groups from getting to know one another better and learning to accept their differences in language, fashion, and religious beliefs. Making matters worse was the outright discrimination displayed against the Chinese immigrants because of their racial characteristics. Most of the Chinese who immigrated to America during the 1800s came from the southern province of Guangdong, China. European immigrants were unaccustomed to their black hair and olive skin tones. Sadly, merely looking different from most other immigrants marked the

Chinese as unacceptable and inferior. Such discrimination led to a lack of trust on both sides.

The California Gold Rush

Chinese immigrants, many of them from peasant families who had rented or owned their own land, were accustomed to toiling long hours on small farm plots in China for little pay (about ten cents a day for an average worker). These immigrants thus went to work wherever there was a need for labor — even "cheap" labor. Cheap by American standards usually equaled far more than the Chinese were used to back home. They heard and read advertisements in China about the

NAMING THE STEREOTYPE AND BREAKING FREE: FROM "ORIENTAL" TO "ASIAN AMERICAN"

Many Chinese Americans have rejected the use of the term "Oriental," a name that has outgrown its early roots in European colonial times. Europeans needed a convenient way to talk about all "Mongoloids," or non-European, Asian cultures, so they decided to group Chinese and other Asian cultures into a general category labeled "Orientals."

When European American immigrants fell on hard times, they chose to blame Chinese immigrants, who were easy targets for discrimination because of their physical and cultural differences. Anti-Chinese sentiment grew, and the term "Oriental" took an ugly turn. Calling someone "Oriental" labeled a person as someone who was not from Europe and not an American, someone who could be blamed for taking away jobs and being a "menace to civilization," an outsider who was not wanted in America.

Other ethnic cultures share a similar history of discrimination and stereotyping, complete with names designed to promote a negative image. For example, African Americans reject old labels such as "Negro," a term that brings back unwanted memories of being slaves to "white" men.

Today, Asian Pacific Americans and Chinese Americans prefer more accurate and positive names such as "Asian American" and "Chinese American." These terms better express the cultural, linguistic, and ethnic diversity of Asian ethnic groups while giving credit for common American historical experiences shared by all Americans.

By taking away the hyphen that used to be part of the terms "Asian-American" and "Chinese-American," Chinese Americans are expressing their complete Chinese and American identities. The name "Chinese American" tells the complete Chinese and American story of a group of people who are no longer foreigners or outsiders in America, their motherland.

higher pay they could earn in America, as much as one to two dollars a day! In their eyes, digging for gold gave them a chance to return home with more wealth than they could ever imagine, had they stayed in China to work.

Sadly, the Chinese miners who came to reap their share of the California gold rush were left to work leftover and undesirable claims where easy-to-find surface ore had already been removed. As the numbers of Chinese miners increased in just two years from five hundred in 1850 to nearly twenty-five thousand in 1852, they came to be seen as an economic threat, because they were taking jobs from Americans. Many Chinese were beaten, robbed, and pushed off their mining fields as a result of fear and discrimination.

As mining itself became more dangerous, many Chinese immigrants entered other occupations such as cooking food, selling supplies, doing laundry, and providing other services for other miners in the work camps. Some opened restaurants and laundry shops to sell food and services to non-Chinese Americans. By the mid-1860s, most of the accessible gold mines were played out, and hopes for a quick fortune were dashed. Still, many Chinese stayed in America and sent a good portion of their earnings home to China.

The Transcontinental Railroad

In the early 1860s, two companies contracted to build the first transcontinental railroad, stretching all the way from the eastern United States to the West Coast. The Union Pacific Railroad was to build westward from Omaha, Nebraska, and the Central Pacific Railroad was to build eastward from Sacramento, California, to create the final section of rail.

By 1864, the Civil War had created a serious U.S. labor shortage. In the West, the Central Pacific Railroad, struggling to complete its portion of the transcontinental railroad, contracted with the Chinese Six Companies to provide workers, many of them captured in China and brought against their will. While at first European immigrants resented the Chinese laborers, they were quickly convinced that the Chinese immigrants were capable of the huge task.

Working under horrendous conditions in a harsh climate and dangerous terrain, they toiled for five years to build what had never been attempted before. At one point, over twelve thousand Chinese immigrants sweated and struggled to tunnel through mountains of granite, cut down forests of dense trees, and bridge cavernous valleys. They worked by hand and with picks, shovels, crowbars, axes, sledgehammers, blasting powder, wheelbarrows, and one-horse dump carts.

Chinese laborers worked long twelve- and fourteen-hour days for a meager wage of less than one dollar per day. Regardless of the freezing cold or broiling sun, they never slowed down. Untold hundreds of Chinese workers died and were buried along the rail line. Only once did they stop working in an attempt to improve their working conditions, but to no avail. Few managers at the Central Pacific Railroad cared about anything other than the money they stood to make when the railroad was completed.

The Golden Spike

Finally, on May 10, 1869, at a celebration at Promontory Point, Utah, the last railroad spike (appropriately made of gold!) was driven into the ground, completing the task begun over six years before. The "Golden Spike" joined the two ends of the transcontinental railroad, marking its completion thanks to the labor, dedication, and lives of many Chinese immigrants.

Yet in spite of the hard work and proven loyalty of the Chinese railroad workers, they were excluded from the official picture and ceremony. Though the supervisor of the CP Railroad had once praised the Chinese for their industrious and devoted work, once the task was completed, not one official word of gratitude or recognition was uttered.

Such treatment by railroad and government officials echoed past discrimination against Chinese immigrants and foreshadowed exclusionary practices to come. The Central Pacific Railroad had always treated Chinese workers differently than the Europeans. While most worker contracts included provisions for food and housing, the

Chinese were not given a place to live and were forced to find their own cooks while working on the railroad.

After the Railroads: From Fisheries to Cigar Factories

After completion of the transcontinental railroad, Chinese immigrant laborers fanned out across the United States in search of work. Many returned to California to work in the agricultural industry, harvesting wheat, fruit, and other crops. They also helped in the construction of some of the first irrigation projects in central California and helped drain swampy lands in the San Joaquin and Sacramento River deltas.

These early Chinese immigrants also worked in the fishing industry, an occupation familiar to many from the coastal regions of

Industrious Chinese laborers found work in California vineyards, pressing grapes. Some even built wine cellars. Many Chinese workers toiled long hours for little pay in railroads, mines, and the agricultural and fishing industries to earn money to support their families left behind in China.

Cultural traditions were kept alive at places like this early-1900s Chinese Opera House in New York's Chinatown. Early immigrants formed Chinatown communities across America.

Arkansas, and other states in the Deep South, while others put in long hours in clothing and shoe factories on the East Coast. Chinese immigrants even worked at rolling cigars, something they had no experience doing since tobacco was not widely grown in China at that time.

And, of course, there were other railroad building projects. Railroad tracks began growing northward from San Francisco and Sacramento, reaching into the Pacific Northwest. Over fifteen thousand Chinese laborers helped build the Northern Pacific Railroad, stretching from Washington state through Idaho and into Montana. More Chinese helped build the Southern Pacific Railroad east from California to Arizona and New Mexico and into Texas.

"Little China"

Ties between Chinese immigrants and their families back home were stretched but not broken as they settled into communities that recreated familiar and valued traditions in food and social customs. When familiar foods were unavailable in America, Chinese immigrants opened stores importing traditional Chinese foods such as canned abalone, mushrooms, bamboo shoots, rice, cuttlefish, and soybean to sell to their own community. While many immigrants found it comforting to settle close to others from their home countries, these sheltered Chinese communities also provided protection from people with anti-Chinese feelings. As the American economy grew worse in the 1870s, anti-

Guangdong Province. These hearty fishermen harvested shrimp, shark, squid, sturgeon, abalone, and flounder, among other types of ocean life.

In other parts of the country, Chinese immigrants worked to gain acceptance as competent and reliable laborers. In the Pacific Northwest, the Chinese were excluded from salmon fishing but were allowed to work in the fish canneries, killing, gutting, and cleaning the fish caught by other fishermen. Some worked in the fields of Arizona,

Chinese feelings grew stronger, putting the Chinese immigrants in danger. Their secluded neighborhood in San Francisco was known first as "Little China," and later other similar communities in cities across the U.S. were called "Chinatowns."

Mostly men emigrated from China to America, with few if any women making the long journey across the Pacific Ocean. Thus, the decision to leave for America meant accepting great change. Chinese immigrants knew they would have to temporarily separate from their families and everything familiar. Wives, mothers, and children back in China would have to learn to do without the family member who played the most important role in the traditional Chinese family structure — the father figure. Yet they believed that somehow their sacrifice would benefit them in the long run.

Kinship Associations

One attempt to maintain a Chinese family and community structure in America was the development of kinship associations, usually located in Chinatown. Based either on family surnames or on geographic or village ties from the old country, such groups helped maintain a strong sense of family despite the absence of women among Chinese immigrants. They also united immigrants from the different regions of China upon their arrival in the United States. The efforts of these family and kinship associations are seen in the concentration of certain

New York's Chinatown continues to serve as home to many new immigrants seeking familiar food, customs, and languages. Modern Chinatowns also attract tourists from many ethnic backgrounds.

Chinese surnames in various regions of the United States. For example, many families with the name Moy and Ng live in the Midwest. At a broader level, district associations helped Chinese from a particular region in the United States bond together as a means of maintaining family harmony even abroad.

With the growth of these various associations, each with its own family or regional loyalties, it was only natural that there would be conflict between the different groups.

Feuding between clan and district associations grew to such a level in the late 1850s that in San Francisco, local association elders organized the "Chung Wai Wui Koon," or "Six Companies," to help iron out problems among the different members. This was the same organization that later provided labor for building the transcontinental railroad.

Foreigners in a Land Built by Immigrants

In areas where many Chinese immigrants settled, discriminatory laws were passed against this hard-working group of people. For example, a 1906 law forbade Chinese children from attending San Francisco public schools with other children, assigning them to segregated "Oriental" public schools instead. Such anti-Chinese laws kept Chinese immigrants socially apart from the mainstream, denying them the same chance to make America their home that other immigrant groups enjoyed.

Adjusting to the different living and working conditions as well as to new food and cooking methods was easy compared to being isolated from other Chinese in America. The life they had left behind in China did not include the dangerous working conditions that awaited them in the mountainous terrain as they built the railroad. Many had lived in small villages where families knew one another and work was done in the open farm fields. In America, the Chinese immigrants were forced to live in crowded and segregated quarters, fearing that their homes and shops would be set afire by other immigrants who blamed them for their troubles.

Segregated though it was, housing in railroad towns became home to work gangs of twelve to fifteen men, with a Chinese chef

A laundry in the early 1900s. Jobs open to the Chinese from the late 1800s throughout the 1900s were often limited to labor-intensive tasks such as laundry work. Laundry, restaurant, and other service shops needed less money to start up and did not pose a threat to non-Chinese workers.

Segregated "Oriental" schools formed when Chinese children were not allowed to attend public schools with other kids from their neighborhoods.

performing duties that made it a little easier for them to be away from their families in China. The cook prepared nutritious meals of fish and vegetables (rather than the beans and beef preferred by other workers). He also boiled water for making tea, general cleaning, and laundering workers' clothes after long hours on the railroad.

With the Recession of 1870, however, things got worse. As more and more European immigrants lost their jobs because of a general downturn in the economy, they became more eager than ever to blame the Chinese for "taking" their jobs. As more and more Americans were left unemployed, the cry went out to restrict the number of Chinese and other Asians allowed to come to America.

"Chinese must go" slogans caught on throughout the West Coast, especially in California, as the economy continued its long slide downward toward America's

Great Depression of 1927. Fires were set to Chinese homes and businesses in street riots. Violence against the Chinese spread throughout San Francisco, forcing many to either return to China or move to the Midwest and East Coast.

When the Chinese Exclusion Act was passed in 1882, Chinese immigrants faced the toughest challenge of any immigrant group. This act prevented Chinese, including wives, children, and other family members, from joining Chinese immigrants in America. It meant that Chinese already living here might not see family members for years — or ever again. While other immigrants freely entered the United States, the Chinese were barred for over sixty years from coming to a country built by immigrants — including the Chinese who, though their numbers were small, made important contributions to their new country. The Chinese Exclusion Act was finally repealed in 1943.

A mother and her baby shop for Chinese produce at a Chinatown fruit and vegetable market in New York. Chinatowns play an important role for many Chinese Americans, providing a place for them to find familiar customs.

CHAPTER THREE

FAMILY AND COMMUNITY LIFE
OLD TIES, NEW TIMES

"**W**hy can't we be more like our friends from school?" grumbles Michael as he bounces his basketball into the back of the garage and tosses his Chinese language books into the car. Mrs. Lee, his mother, is in the driver's seat. She is rushing to get Michael, thirteen, and his nine-year-old sister, Sarah, to a church a few miles away to attend Chinese language school with other Chinese American children. They meet for a couple of hours every day after their regular school.

Even though Michael and Sarah like their new friends in language school, attending this class prevents them from taking part in sports, joining clubs, and participating in other after-school activities they might enjoy. Michael spends a few more hours each evening after dinner doing both his regular and language-school homework. Sarah doesn't have as much homework, but she does spend extra hours practicing with the Chinese Folk Dance Team at the church, which she enjoys.

While these special ethnic cultural activities set Sarah and Michael apart from many of their school friends, required attendance at the Chinese language school to learn ancestral customs and languages is common in Chinese American households. This is especially true in first- and second-generation Chinese American families.

Traditional Family Values
Link the Past and Future

For Chinese Americans who hold on tightly to traditions and "old world" values, the family is the most important part of life. Preserving the best from one generation to the next starts at home, where lessons learned

Sharing a meal is an important part of family life in most Chinese American homes.

WHICH GENERATION AMERICAN ARE YOU?

The Lee family first settled in America when great-grandfather Lee immigrated in the early 1900s. Their children, including Sarah and Michael's grandfather on their father's side, became the family's first generation of Chinese Americans because they were the first children born in America. Sarah and Michael's grandmother on their father's side immigrated a few years later, after marrying their grandfather in China. Grandmother Lee was able to join her husband in 1945, after the War Bride's Act was passed, allowing wives of war veterans to reunite with their husbands. Their mother's family has a similar history; Sarah and Michael's maternal grandparents are also first-generation Chinese Americans. This makes Sarah and Michael's parents part of the second generation of Chinese Americans in both families, and Sarah and Michael are third-generation Chinese Americans.

from grandparents, great-grandparents and great-great-grandparents are not forgotten. Parents pass along cultural values to their children, and for traditional Chinese households, the family unit is central to all individual and community activities. Lessons learned in the family are considered the key to realizing the dreams of past and future generations.

For example, family elders tell stories about their life and relationships with their mothers, fathers, brothers, and sisters. They may share memories of their lives in old China and their hard journey to achieve a better life here in America. Sharing memories of a parent's experiences as a teenager during different times bonds younger generations of Chinese Americans with older ones. It also creates a feeling of appreciation from one generation to the next. Learning about a father's childhood in America, when he may have worked long hours after school to earn enough money to send back to his mother in China, gives insight into how different and difficult life could be for earlier Chinese immigrants, especially compared to the better life many Chinese parents have given their American-born children. Chinese parents may also use stories describing their lives of physical labor to convince their children of the importance of a good education.

A Strong Family Structure

As in other traditional American families, parents provide economic and emotional support in the

A vegetable seller's family unloads their produce at the market. The importance of the family is carried from home to work.

COMFORTS OF LOVE: THE FAMILY COAT

Michael and Sarah's great-grandfather tells the story of his journey to America in the early 1900s. Great-grandfather Lee's father had returned to China after first leaving his family in China to work on the Central Pacific Railroad. Having seen more opportunities in America, he arranged for his son, great-grandfather Lee, to travel to New York and work for his brother's restaurant there. At the age of sixteen, great-grandfather Lee prepared to leave his mother, father, and two brothers for a strange, faraway country. Familiar with the colder climate in America, the boy's father instructed his son to pack extra blankets. He packed several cotton quilts and a small amount of clothes in the one bag he was allowed to bring onto the ship.

On the day of his son's departure, great-great-grandfather Lee gave his son some-thing that had already traveled across the Pacific Ocean from China to America, and back again — a heavy winter coat he had worn in his journeys to and from America. Young and afraid, the boy wrapped his father's coat around him, picked up his suitcase, and bravely boarded the ship that would trace the path his father had taken earlier.

The coat comforted him, physically and emotionally. In spite of the miles that would separate great-grandfather Lee from his family in China, he knew that he would be watched over.

Michael and Sarah watched the tears of joy well up in great-grandfather Lee's eyes after he shared this childhood memory with them. And then they gave him a big hug, grateful for the family coat that had kept him safe and warm on his trip to America.

typical Chinese American home. In the past, Chinese practicing strict Confucian religion saw the family, the father and mother, children and their aunts, uncles, and cousins, as a separate and highly structured unit, much like the government. In addition to these relatives, the family in China often included other village members, thereby extending the authority of the family beyond its blood members. Even today, the belief in a strong and self-contained family over other groupings makes many Asian American households different from European American households.

For example, even younger Chinese American homes reflect the value of working hard to keep the family together, often by sacrificing individual goals in order to main-tain family unity. One or both parents will work to support the high cost of putting their children through the best schools and universities and to pay the mortgage, health care, and other household bills. Children are expected to pitch in with the housework and also make enough time for schoolwork. Grandparents, aunts, uncles, and cousins try to live near one another, strengthening the family bond.

In comparison, family members in many European cultures are raised to be more independent from the family. For example, while a European American might not hesitate to go outside the family to borrow money, members of a traditional Chinese American home believe that all monetary and emotional needs should be met from within the closed family structure. Asking "strangers" for money would be considered a slight to the family.

Family Roles and Modern Society

Chinese American households must react to many of the same challenges facing their non-Chinese neighbors and friends, but they tend to place greater importance on putting the family first, before individual needs. This is especially true of newer Chinese immigrant families and those living in Chinatowns, where family members may still speak Chinese rather than English.

For many of these families, as for other older and more traditional American homes, preserving native customs and values is a way to maintain order and comfort in a modern society that may seem ever-changing or even threatening.

While divorce and single-parent families are not unusual in America today, they are less common in traditional Chinese American households. Since traditional Chinese families still believe that the good of the family as a whole is more important than the needs of any one parent or child, these families may work harder to avoid the breakdown of the traditional family structure. Parents will often sacrifice personal happiness —

which may mean avoiding separating or divorce — to keep the family together.

Changes in Traditional Male and Female Roles

Though men have traditionally held a higher place in the Chinese family hierarchy, Chinese American families today reflect more contemporary views of male and female equality. Gone are the days when mothers stayed home to care for the children while fathers worked outside the home to support the family. If mothers worked in China, they worked on the family farm, and their incomes supplemented their husbands' earnings. Today, parents set a different example, with both father and mother working inside and outside the home in professional as well as clerical and manual labor jobs. Like many other Americans, both parents must work to ensure bright futures for their sons and daughters. Many younger Chinese Americans find it hard to imagine a time when fathers could be the only wage earner.

In traditional Chinese homes, the first-born son was responsible for fulfilling Confucian obligations by caring for his parents after they retired and supporting his relatives. In Chinese American families today, daugh-

RESPECT FOR ELDERS SURVIVES YEARS OF DISCRIMINATION

Many first- and some second-generation Chinese Americans grew up without daily contact with their grandparents, who were kept from coming to America by anti-Chinese immigration laws. Many relatives, including wives and mothers, were separated from their families by these laws. Despite the absence of older people in many families,

the Confucian belief in honoring elders in the community has been carried forward to Chinese American life today.

Though young Chinese Americans today may not believe in some traditional Chinese customs themselves, they often follow them out of respect for their older relatives.

ters are valued equally to sons, and sons are rarely favored over daughters as heirs to the family name and honor as they were in ancient Chinese times.

Women have traditionally played an important role in Chinese American families, caring for the children and making home life as comfortable as possible despite the early history of hardship and isolation from other families caused by cultural barriers. Though still not as visible as men in today's Chinese American family, women have earned respect and equality by working behind the scenes, saving to buy a house or family business, planning for a child's education, and caring for all family members. In addition to contributing to the family's well-being by working in the outside world, the mother is often the glue that holds the family together.

Born Out of Necessity: The Extended Family

Extended families became necessary during the 1800s and early 1900s when immediate families were kept an ocean apart by anti-Chinese laws and policies. In addition to the Chinese Exclusion Act, which barred Chinese laborers and their wives from coming to the United States, other laws did not allow American citizens to marry the Chinese, taking away their citizenship if they did. And to further prevent the start of new Chinese families, Chinese women were barred from entering the country.

Prior to World War II, Chinese men and the few Chinese women living in America endured racism and fear by forming family associations made up of people with the same last name (see Chapter Two). Also, Chinese men who were forced to live miles apart from their wives and children depended on "Bachelor Societies," clubs where men supported one another financially and emotionally, while hoping to be reunited with their families. These extended families played a needed role by helping the Chinese find jobs and loans to survive during difficult economic times. Most family associations were located in Chinatowns or other communities made up of Chinese immigrants.

When the Chinese Exclusion Act was repealed in 1943, only 105 Chinese were given permission to come to America annually until 1965. Even at that slow rate, families were eventually reunited, and today they have become the extended families of new immigrants who are themselves without relatives or a network of social support.

The Changing Role of Chinatowns

Chinatowns came into existence in the 1920s and 1930s when early Chinese immigrants settled in a neighborhood to be close to other immigrants. Living among their Chinese neighbors comforted new immigrant families, who shared more than street names. Chinatown residents were able to speak their native Chinese languages and practice familiar customs.

Today, new Chinese immigrants may still settle and work in the Chinatowns located in several major American cities. Chinatown is also a place where second-, third-, and fourth-generation Chinese Americans may sample some of their history and culture. Shopping for authentic Chinese foods, toys, crafts, and gifts with family and friends is a fun way to share some of their Chinese American history.

While Chinatown is an interesting place for Chinese Americans to introduce their culture to friends, gone is the sense that families need to live close to other Chinese families in order to rediscover their own

New York City's skyline peers over a Chinatown ice-cream factory. The homes and jobs of modern Chinese American families are no longer limited to Chinatown boundaries.

cultural "roots." Today, Chinese American families are comfortable living in many different areas of the country, in diverse neighborhoods regardless of the number of Chinese neighbors. Like most Americans, they want safe and friendly neighborhoods with the best schools and nearby churches and stores. Parents believe that just as it is important to preserve family values and traditions, it is also important to give their children educational opportunities and the luxuries of a good American life often found in suburban locations outside Chinatown communities.

Reinforcing Family Values with Community Involvement

Chinese American community life is an extension of the close family structure. By making friends with other Chinese American children through language school and other community activities, young people discover that their family experiences are normal. Knowing that Chinese American friends hear the same tales and traditions in their families, too, makes grandmother's old Chinese customs seem not so strange after all.

Traditional customs are passed along to Chinese American children through Chinese community organizations that sponsor get-togethers, dinners, parties, and language schools. As we have seen in the experience of Michael and Sarah, these Chinese language schools take place after regular school hours and sometimes make for a long day. But they offer an opportunity for many Chinese American youth to learn how to read, write, and speak Mandarin or Cantonese, the two major Chinese dialects.

Colorfully costumed youth dancers perform a traditional fan dance at a Chinese New Year banquet. Many Chinese communities host festive holiday celebrations, complete with dance troupes.

In addition to learning their parents' or grandparents' native language, many Chinese American children are taught Chinese folk dances. The girls participate in colorful Chinese ribbon, fan, chopsticks, and hoop dances, donning festive outfits and performing at traditional holiday celebrations. Boys practice moves for the dragon and lion dances and perform during Chinese New Year parades or parties. Martial arts such as Kung Fu or Tai Chi Chuan are sometimes taught in the community.

Children's Education as the Key to Advancement

Michael Lee wonders, "Why do I have to always finish my homework?" and toys with the idea of closing his books and going out to shoot a few baskets with his friends.

Michael, and other Chinese Americans like him, often take for granted their parents'

active interest in their schoolwork. Ancient Confucian values dictated that education was the key to advancement in life. The various dynasties that ruled China used education as a means of separating the elite from the masses. It was nearly always the case in ancient China that the wealthy who could afford to educate their children were perceived as having great power and influence. This historical framework was key in the minds of immigrants who came to America seeking their fortunes. They generally were not wealthy. But they took advantage of the chance to educate their young so the children could rise to power and influence. In essence, education became the great equalizer for the Chinese in America.

A strong interest in education still characterizes Chinese American culture today. Parents actively support their children's academic progress by spending time helping

A young girl practices her Chinese calligraphy by tracing characters with ink and a Chinese brush. Many young Chinese Americans attend Chinese language school after regular school.

with homework assignments and, when necessary, hiring tutors to coach children in difficult subjects. Even some of the best students receive help from tutors and parents to prepare them for college entrance exams.

Dating and Marriage in the Traditional Chinese American Family

Most traditional Chinese parents prefer that their Chinese American children date and marry other Chinese Americans who share similar cultural values. Many of these parents view marriage outside the Chinese culture as a threat to preserving family togetherness and values. They believe that marrying

someone who shares similar views on religion, raising children, education, money, and politics forms a solid foundation for a long-lasting family network.

Some second-, third-, and even fourth-generation Chinese Americans still hold a strong commitment to preserving their rich cultural past through marriage and family life. Even though society no longer pressures them to marry within the same race, some Chinese Americans prefer marrying others who share similar bicultural experiences and values.

Sarah and Michael's parents were introduced by family friends. Because they were born in America, they had adopted many Western views on dating and marriage. Both dated inside and outside the Chinese American community. But although they had not restricted their dating to Asians alone, they were attracted to each other when they met because they shared many things, including their cultural roots. Their decision to marry was for them, as it is for most American couples, a personal choice. And yet, like many Americans of a certain religious or ethnic background, their decision was also based on family as well as individual values and expectations.

Mixed-Race Dating and Marriages

Parents like Mr. and Mrs. Lee realize that children growing up in American cities and towns may not have the opportunity to meet and date only Chinese Americans. Learning to appreciate and accept their unique ethnic and cultural heritage is more important for a growing number of Chinese Americans today.

Mixed-race or interracial dating between Chinese Americans and European Americans, African Americans, Japanese Americans, and others is on the rise. According to a recent U.S. Census, about two million children live in multiracial households, with the largest group living in mixed Asian-European American households. Rather than placing limits on their dating choices, many more Americans are learning to value friendships with Americans from all ethnic cultures, knowing that when it comes time to marry,

their choices will be as varied as Americans themselves, and each relationship unique.

A Strong Work Ethic in the Family Structure

Many newer Chinese American immigrant families living in Chinatown communities work long hours in restaurants and clothing factories, struggling to fulfill their Confucian duty to support their relatives. Outside these mostly first-generation Chinese American communities, other Chinese American parents also carry on the traditional work ethic, working hard at many different careers to pay for good housing, food, and education for their families.

This commitment to work hard and do your best at any task is a value learned and adopted from ancestors who endured hardship in China years ago. Even today, people living in China see limited opportunities for good schooling and jobs compared to what's available in America. Chinese American parents remind their children of this difference

A Chinese noodle factory, one of many businesses started by immigrants for their community. Many remain in Chinatown districts.

THE CHINESE LAUNDRY: AN EXAMPLE OF THE WORK ETHIC

Early Chinese immigrants labored as miners during the California gold rush, workers on the transcontinental railroad, or launderers for European immigrant workers. When the Chinese Exclusion Act of 1882 was repealed in 1943, Chinese immigrants were again allowed to come to America. But the only businesses they were allowed to open were those that served the needs of largely European immigrants while posing little threat to the livelihoods of those immigrants. Laundries, restaurants, and other small service shops were among the businesses that fit this category and these were the businesses started by many Chinese immigrants.

So even though they probably did not own laundries in China or prefer this type of work, many Chinese immigrants who arrived during and after World War II settled in Chinatowns and became launderers.

Industrious and hard working, Chinese immigrants overcame legal discrimination and anti-Chinese feelings to earn a living and provide for their families here and overseas. Today, few "hand laundries" exist, thanks to the invention of commercial and home washing machines and clothes dryers. In their place are thousands of businesses of all types founded by Chinese Americans, fueled by pride and a strong work ethic.

to help them see the importance of developing good work attitudes and habits.

Those growing up in Chinese American family businesses experience this work ethic firsthand. Fathers and mothers work long hours and sometimes sacrifice leisure time. Many families combine spending time together with working in the family business, owning and operating retail stores, restaurants, printing shops, trade companies, and tailoring, laundry, and dry cleaning services. But more important than the type of business owned by Chinese American families is their pride and commitment to working together to achieve success.

Cultural Conflict and the Model Minority Myth

Children raised in Chinese American families, like most ethnic minority groups in America, struggle to understand both their Chinese and American identities. They may experience pressures to choose between tradi-

tional "Eastern" Chinese backgrounds and the less traditional "Western" lifestyle of their other American friends. Eastern cultures differ from many of America's Western ways. It is common for children from immigrant and traditional ethnic families to experience some confusion when faced with the question of which group they actually belong to.

Pressured to succeed at school, sports, and other activities inside and outside the home, Chinese American youth face additional demands by simply being Chinese. Thanks in part to these pressures from within their own community, and thanks in part to the images that have been drawn of them by people outside their community, Chinese American kids have become stereotyped as a "model minority."

A stereotype is a belief formed about a group of people based on an overly simplified set of traits. People tend to form stereotypes, both positive and negative, in an attempt to learn about something foreign to them.

However, people who rely on stereotyping do not learn enough to really understand either individuals or their culture. Stereotyping portrays all members of a group as identical, overlooking individual differences due to either ethnic background or personality. As a result, stereotypes often pit one group against another.

A Chinese American teenager talks with his teacher. Like most American youth, Chinese Americans face increasing pressures and need support and guidance from family and community.

Since many early Chinese immigrants were hardworking, industrious, and bright, overcoming the obstacles of a foreign country that did not welcome them, they earned a reputation as a "model minority." This stereotype continues today, affecting Chinese Americans of all ages and backgrounds.

As a group, Chinese American youth represent a large number of the country's best colleges and universities. But on closer examination, the "model minority" stereotype is a myth. Though some Chinese Americans appear to fit the mold of perfect students, bound to excel at whatever they do, they face the same demands and desires as other Americans their age. If teachers expect them to rise above any difficulty without the special attention given to other immigrant students, Chinese Americans can suffer from being marked as superior. Making things worse, teachers and parents may compare other young people to these "super minority" kids, unintentionally making them the target of scorn by others who resent their perfect image.

Chinese Americans suffer many of the same problems that have always faced American-born children of immigrants. Rebelling against the added pressures from their parents' and others' high expectations of them, some Chinese American youth find themselves alienated from their parents. Others find themselves turning against the institutions, such as church and school, that have traditionally encouraged them to succeed. In cities with large Asian American populations, some kids have buckled under the pressure and joined youth gangs, just as other American kids give in to peer pressure and make unwise personal choices. Ironically, in their efforts to cope with the often jumbled expectations of family, community, and peer groups, Chinese American youth have shown how much like other American kids they actually are.

A chief priest at a Buddhist temple. Chinese American belief systems are influenced by Buddhism, Taoism, Confucianism, and Christianity.

CHAPTER FOUR

RELIGION AND CELEBRATIONS
A BLENDING OF FAITHS

Chinese Americans follow a long tradition of working hard to keep the family together, with the kind of devotion that others reserve for religious faith. In fact, the Chinese American tie to the family may be stronger than its ties to any one organized religion. Many second-, third-, and fourth-generation Chinese Americans unknowingly blend ancient Chinese beliefs with new ones adopted from Western cultures. For example, in recognizing Easter, a Christian celebration, the Lee family blends Western and Eastern religious and cultural belief systems.

Eastern Beliefs in a Western World

Michael and Sarah eagerly await their hunt for the candy-filled baskets that their mother hides from them every Easter Sunday. But first they must go to church and then, with other family members, visit great-grandfather's grave at a gravesite bought by one of the Chinese churches for the Chinese community. At great-grandfather's tombstone, their grandfather places fresh flowers and long sticks of burning incense (*ja guaun*) to honor a member of the family's ancestry. Then each family member takes turns bowing three times in front of the grave to show respect. The eldest bows first, followed by the others according to age.

Michael and Sarah's mother and father tell stories of their own childhood when they practiced the same Easter tradition as first-generation Chinese Americans but also offered food to their grandfather's "ghost" in the Buddhist tradition. Feeding the souls of ancestors is believed to show that family members have not forgotten the well-being of their dead relatives, honoring their duty to care for family even beyond this life.

Chinese Buddhists believe in an active spirit world, remembering a long line of ancestors who have influence over the physical world. In addition to bowing and placing burning sticks of incense in homage to the dead, Chinese Buddhists offer food to dead ancestors at their gravesites, honoring them

Incense is burned and flowers placed at graves to honor dead ancestors during Qing Ming Day, the Chinese Memorial Day.

with their favorite meal when they were living. This is part of the Buddhist observance honoring ancestors each spring during the Chinese Memorial Day (Qing Ming). Well-fed and remembered ancestors are happy, looking after the family and possibly giving health and returned happiness to the living.

While Christians also pay visits to the graves of loved ones, Chinese American families may not necessarily share all of the religious beliefs of their non-Chinese neighbors. Faith and hope play an important role in the Chinese American family, but joining organized religion in the form of church membership is no more important than having a strong set of beliefs and values. Traditional Chinese culture has always sought religion in the whole life, rather than confining it to any activity called "church."

The Chinese Community Church

Though many nineteenth-century Chinese immigrants did not identify with any one religion, upon their arrival in America they were exposed to Christianity. Today, the Christian church is a regular part of life for most Americans, including Chinese Americans, and many more Chinese Americans are Christians than Buddhists. Local Chinese churches historically have played an important role for many Chinese immigrants looking to the Chinese Community Church for friendship, social and health services, and spiritual support.

With English as their second language, earlier Chinese Americans did not feel comfortable socializing beyond their immediate family and Chinese-speaking friends. Many would only leave their homes to work, getting

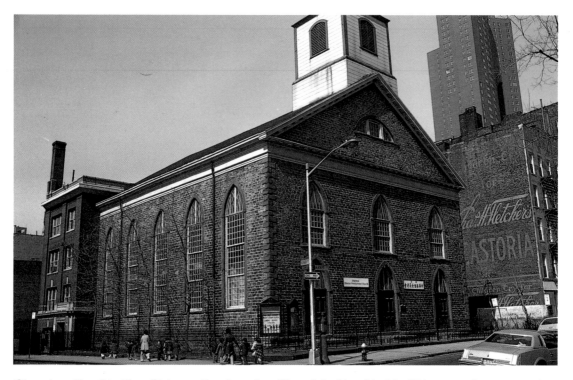

Churches like this First Chinese Presbyterian Church in New York's Chinatown have served as more than a place of worship for many Chinese Americans. They continue to play a large role in Chinese American communities.

by with just enough English to shop for the family's basic food needs and supplies. Chinese Community Churches offered English language classes for immigrants, where they also recruited students to attend Sunday services. Some families sent their children to Sunday school specifically to meet other Chinese Americans. The church became a second home to many new immigrant families and a way to meet other Chinese-speaking people also looking for a place to learn English without fear of rejection.

While Chinese Community Churches across the United States still play this important role for new immigrants, much like an extended family, they have become a mainstay for many established Chinese American communities as well. Second- and third-generation Chinese American families continue to bring their children to the church where they grew up, making the Chinese Community Church a big part of their regular schedule of activities. Today the role of church-sponsored language school has been reversed; rather than sending their American-born children to learn English, younger Chinese American parents enroll their children in Chinese language classes.

Chinese Moral Values and American Religious Tradition

Many people from Asian cultures, including the Chinese, are strongly influenced by the three ancient religions of China: Buddhism, Confucianism, and Taoism. In contrast, most American ideas about morality and ethics come from traditional Christian beliefs. These beliefs were brought to America by the first European settlers; many, like the Pilgrims, came to the colonies fleeing religious persecution at the hands of the English Crown.

When Chinese immigrants first started coming to America in the early 1800s, Christianity was not widespread in Asia. The earliest immigrants from China, therefore, did not share the Christian beliefs of their European counterparts. However, the second-largest wave of Chinese immigrants, which began arriving in the 1940s, had already been influenced by Christian missionaries in China and other parts of Asia.

The blending of Eastern and Western religious ideas was made easier for immigrants by the fact that many of their beliefs roughly paralleled Judeo-Christian values. For example, the Chinese rule of respect for elders sounds a lot like the commandment to "honor thy father and thy mother." The taking of human life was not allowed by either Christian or Chinese beliefs. And the Chinese philosopher Confucius had a slightly different version of the so-called golden rule to do to others what you would have them do to you: "Don't do to others what you wouldn't want them to do to you."

Big differences remained, however, between Chinese religions and Christianity. For example, the Chinese had no restriction on polygamy, the practice of having more than one husband or wife. And organized religion plays a much less powerful role in shaping Chinese moral values and tradition than religion in the West and the Islamic world. Elements of all three Chinese faiths — Buddhism, Confucianism, and Taoism — may be practiced by the same family; together they shape the traditional Chinese belief system that is the heritage of Chinese Americans. But over time, Eastern beliefs and values, being less rigid than many religions and lacking organizations dedicated to perpetuating them, have been adapted to fit in with traditional Western laws and religions.

Buddhism

Buddhism began in India and spread to Southeast Asia, where it was adopted by the Chinese several hundred years before the birth of Christ. Buddhists see life as endless suffering and believe that after death, one is reincarnated, or reborn as another form of life. Buddhists strive to break out of the reincarnation cycle by living a life more virtuous than the previous one.

Followers of this religion believe it is necessary to give up any attachment to material or worldly things in order to find peace and happiness in a simpler way of life. Buddhists would frown upon buying children expensive toys or clothes, preferring to pass along Buddhist values like getting by in life with only basic necessities. Rather than attempt to keep up with changing fashions, Buddhists would teach children that the goal of getting new clothes is to keep up with their growth spurts.

Confucianism and Taoism

Today's Chinese Americans are still influenced by the teachings of two ancient Chinese philosophers, Confucius and Lao-Tze. While many consider Confucianism and Taoism to be religions like Buddhism, others view them as philosophies or codes of ethics. Philosophers are scholars who teach society rules to live by through the development and examination of principles and beliefs.

Confucius was a philosopher known for his sensible yet idealistic advice and beliefs that affect people's lives even today. Confucian beliefs underlie many Chinese customs and traditions; family togetherness, respect

A Chinese American child worships at the Buddhist altar in her home. While Christianity is the dominant religion in America, long-established Eastern religions like Buddhism are also practiced.

for elders, and obedience to authority are still taught in Chinese American families and influence life in modern society.

In the Confucian tradition, parents are seen as the "rulers," or heads of the household, and children are the "people," or those serving the ruler (and served by the ruler). Though young couples may not agree with the older customs and conservative ways of their elders, out of respect they will obey the wishes of their parents and grandparents.

But many modern Chinese Americans from the second or third generation see themselves as Westerners with a different outlook than that of their Eastern ancestors. While they accept the Eastern Confucian beliefs in friendship, honor, trust, kindness, education, and proper behavior, these are tempered by opposing beliefs in self-expression and independence from the family.

Taoism was founded by the Chinese philosopher Lao-Tze, and his teachings have been a part of the Chinese culture for over two thousand years. Taoism teaches that humankind needs to find harmony by returning to natural ways of life. It stresses harmony between individuals and nature, concentrating on a good life on earth based on simplicity, naturalness, and peace of mind. Those who practice Taoism avoid all forms of confrontation. Tao means "the way" or "the path" — an understanding of how the universe works.

Chinese Mythology in Modern Society: Traditional Celebrations

Ancient Chinese mythology finds its way into modern Chinese American homes through traditional celebrations and festivals. Some Chinese Americans who believe that fate and luck play a big role in their lives observe traditional customs closely, while

A copper engraving of Confucius, the philosopher who founded Confucianism, the tradition named after him.

THE CHINESE SYMBOL OF THE *TAO*

The Chinese symbol of the *Tao* shows the interplay of two forces: *yin* and *yang*. Yang represents the light, active, positive forces of nature, which Taoists associate with masculinity, while yin represents the opposite — the dark, passive, cold, moist, negative forces that Taoism associates with femininity. Taoist philosophers believe that balancing these battling forces achieves harmony, through which the two renew each other. The circle means that yin and yang follow a cycle, working together rather than against each other to form a circle of harmony and peace.

others follow family and social customs unaware of their rich mythical and mystical histories. The festive and colorful celebrations by Chinese Americans across America leave little doubt that Chinese mythology has transcended the miles and years from ancient China to modern America.

Chinese Lunar New Year

Many people from ancient Asian cultures celebrate the new year based on the lunar calendar rather than the Gregorian calender used in Western nations. According to the lunar calendar, which is based on the moon's revolutions around the earth, the new year usually falls in late January or early February on the Western calendar, which is based on the earth's revolutions around the sun. Following ancient as well as newer traditions, Chinese American families and communities benefit by celebrating the new year twice.

Sarah proudly collects toys, T-shirts, key chains, and anything with a rabbit on it. At last count, she owned nearly thirty stuffed miniature and large toy rabbits, many given to her as birthday gifts from her parents, grandparents, aunts, and uncles. She teases her brother Michael about being a "rat," to which he replies, "Rats are charming and thrifty, and I'm proud to be one!" Growing up in a traditional Chinese American household, they learned early in their lives about the animal symbol connected to the year in which they were born.

The practice of computing time by the lunar calendar, symbolized by twelve different animals, dates as far back as the first century A.D. Each of the twelve annual cycles in the lunar calendar has an animal assigned to it, symbolizing the "personality" and fortune for the year ahead. According to ancient Chinese mythology, everyone should know

THE LUNAR CALENDAR AND THE TWELVE ANIMAL SIGNS

A complete lunar cycle takes sixty years and is made up of five cycles of twelve years each. According to Chinese legend, the Lord Buddha called all the animals to come bid him farewell before he left the earth. When only twelve animals answered his call, he rewarded them by

If you were born in the years:

					Your Chinese lunar animal sign is:
1948	1960	1972	1984	1996	The RAT
1949	1961	1973	1985	1997	The OX
1950	1962	1974	1986	1998	The TIGER
1951	1963	1975	1987	1999	The RABBIT
1952	1964	1976	1988	2000	The DRAGON
1953	1965	1977	1989	2001	The SNAKE
1954	1966	1978	1990	2002	The HORSE
1955	1967	1979	1991	2003	The SHEEP
1956	1968	1980	1992	2004	The MONKEY
1957	1969	1981	1993	2005	The ROOSTER
1958	1970	1982	1994	2006	The DOG
1959	1971	1983	1995	2007	The BOAR

the animal sign under which he or she was born, because knowing that animal's strengths and weaknesses helps chart a life of good fortune.

Every Chinese New Year, Chinese Americans celebrate with family, friends, food, and traditional festivities. Depending on the size of the Chinese American community where they live, celebrations may be small, with family members only, or large and elaborate, complete with a big street parade and noisy firecrackers. And, of course, everyone comes together for an authentic Chinese dinner banquet with family and friends to beckon in the new year. The elaborate meal may include plenty of beef and poultry dishes, including velvet chicken, which is reserved for celebrations and special occasions, and Peking roasted duck. Either shark's fin soup or bird's nest soup is served, both delicacies for the Chinese. Glutinous foods, such as duck's

feet, may be served if older Chinese are present. Duck eggs preserved in tea, served with marinated sweet scallions, are also a delicacy. The seemingly endless variety of dishes includes cold marinated vegetable salads and fresh whole steamed fish in delicious Chinese sauces.

Chinese civic and community organizations may organize a special gala event at a Chinese restaurant or hall, where hundreds from the community watch the dragon and lions perform their dances among the crowd. The dragon is the Chinese symbol for vitality, and the lions represent the protector of humankind and have been present at all celebrations since the Manchu dynasty. The celebration usually takes place the night before the first day of the new year. Houses are cleaned inside and out, leaving everything bright and sparkling for the new year. No sweeping is allowed on New Year's Day, lest any good luck be swept out the door.

naming a lunar year after each one in the order that they arrived. Some believe that the animal ruling the year in which you were born exercises a profound influence on your life. As the Chinese say, "This is the animal that hides in your heart." Below are the twelve lunar animal signs.

Some possible characteristics:

Easy to get along with, hardworking, thrifty; usually bright, happy, sociable; most sentimental of the cycle.
Will achieve fortune through strength and hard work; steady and trustworthy but sometimes naive.
Often colorful, unpredictable; loves being center of attention; able to convince others; warm and sensitive.
Usually peaceful, gracious, and very lucky; may do well in careers in law, politics, and government.
Often fearless, decisive, and full of imagination, especially when others believe in him or her.
The deepest thinkers in the Chinese lunar cycle, valuing honesty, a sense of humor, and responsibility.
Cheerful, popular, and headstrong; may be moody, needing self-expression.
Seen as the Good Samaritans of the cycle; sincere and like helping others in need; often lucky.
Inheriting most of humanity's intelligence; clever, good with language, and sociable.
Often misunderstood, witty, and amusing; like being in the limelight.
The most likable of all in the lunar cycle; honest and intelligent with a deep sense of loyalty and fairness.
Seeks harmony in the world; honest, courageous; very good listener.

Lion dancers parade in a Chinatown street, a familiar scene during Chinese New Year celebrations in many Chinese American communities.

All family members wear new clothes for the new year, signifying a new beginning. The new beginning also applies to personal and business money matters, so any old debts are supposed to be repaid before the new year begins. In many traditional Chinese American households, parents and grandparents prepare "lucky money" in little red envelopes, called *hong bow* in Cantonese, which they present to unmarried children as a symbol of their care and provision for them. Parents consider themselves responsible for all their unmarried children. In turn, children bow to the elders, showing their respect, love, and caring.

Honoring Ancestral Gods

Early Chinese immigrants who settled in Chinatowns practiced a folk religion that also blended the beliefs of the Buddhist, Confucian, and Taoist religions and philosophies. They built altars to honor the gods they worshiped back in China, including Kwang Kung, god of literature and war; Bak Ti, god of the north; Hou Yin, the monkey god; and Kwan Yin, goddess of mercy. Temples were built in each Chinatown serving as places of worship as well as gathering places for celebrations and festivals such as the Lunar New Year, Qing Ming (Memorial Day), and the Moon Festival.

Younger Chinese Americans not living in these mainly first-generation communities treat these ancient Chinese customs as magical superstitions, novel and entertaining in modern America. Influenced by Western advances in science and technology, today's Chinese Americans may balk at practices

such as burning incense or kneeling at a temple, or shaking a container filled with numbered wooden sticks in order to foresee their future. They go along with such strange activities for entertainment, much as they might give in to the temptation to have their palms read at a carnival.

Traditional Chinese may not literally believe in ancestral worship, but some continue to observe the rituals, including family feasts during certain holidays like Qing Ming, the Chinese Memorial Day, which usually falls in March or April. This is a day to honor ancestors by burning paper money or offering food. Just as food is central in many Chinese celebrations, like the New Year banquet, honoring dead ancestors must also include food. In the Buddhist tradition, the ritual is based on belief in an afterlife from which ancestors

These girls are celebrating the Chinese New Year at a community feast. Food plays a big part in many Chinese celebrations and holidays.

look out for the well-being of living family members, as long as they are fed and paid!

Not many Chinese Americans adhere strictly to these practices today. Only at traditional non-Christian Chinese funerals will you find family members honoring "guardian" ancestors by throwing paper money into the grave of the deceased to increase the ancestor's wealth in the afterlife and offering food to guard against hunger and pain. An interesting contradiction in traditional Chinese beliefs is the reluctance to speak of death and dying in spite of the history of ancestor worship. To speak of death and dying is considered bad luck for the living. For many younger Chinese Americans growing up in a Christian society, these beliefs are as foreign as they are to many other Americans. But the Chinese teach tolerance for all religions, something valuable for all cultures.

The Mid-Autumn Moon Festival

Next to the Chinese New Year celebration, the most popular festival still widely celebrated by Chinese Americans today is the mid-autumn Moon Festival, held on the fifteenth day of the eighth month in the lunar calendar. Like harvest festivals in other cultures, including Thanksgiving Day, the Chinese Moon Festival is a time for family and friends to gather and give thanks for the abundance of the season. Similar in purpose to Thanksgiving Day, the Moon Festival is held in late September or early October, according to the lunar calendar.

Many Chinese American communities celebrate by feasting, dancing, and sharing a Chinese snack appropriately named "moon cakes." Moon cakes are thick pastries filled with sweet bean paste, sometimes mixed with nuts and a salted cooked egg inside.

The moon cakes hold an important place in Chinese history; they were used to deliver messages to villagers in a plot to overthrow the Yuan dynasty in the 1300s. Small slips of paper with secret messages on them were placed in the moon cakes and delivered to the rebels. With the moon at its fullest and brightest, the plotters were able to read the

FENG SHUI: SUPERSTITION, ART, OR SCIENCE?

Feng shui (pronounced "fung shway") is the Chinese practice of arranging natural and manufactured objects in a balanced way to create harmonious homes, offices, parks, buildings, and rooms, imparting good health and wealth to the dwellers in these places. Developed over thousands of years of Chinese civilization, Feng shui is considered by its believers a cross between art and science. Feng shui consultants tell home buyers which houses to avoid based on their floor plans. For example, a home with the front door positioned directly in line with the back door would be a bad buy according to Feng shui, because it would allow good spirits that enter the house to go straight out again.

Chinese Americans may or may not believe in this "art," depending on their cultural background. While four out of five Hong Kong-born Chinese are said to follow Feng shui, second- or third-generation Chinese Americans may be much less likely to embrace it. Increasingly, however, Westerners find Feng shui appealing and interest from non-Chinese Americans is on the rise.

messages by its light and carry out their duties.

In parts of China, the moon is thought to bring out the best of the yin, or female, elements of the Tao, in which yin is balanced with yang, the male elements of nature. Chinese folklore tells of villagers dancing around a bonfire, worshiping the moon. Since yin is associated with the dark, worshiping the moon promotes its brightness, helping to bring out the best of the dark sky. The yin elements are described as solid, dark, cool, quiescent, growth-sustaining, responsive, and feminine.

Today, the Moon Festival is a time for family reunions and sharing a meal with friends in a large community banquet hall, at the park, or at friends' homes. It is a time for looking up at the moon while folk stories are passed on to children. It is a time to remember our past, giving thanks, yet looking forward to the next "crop" and hoping for abundance.

Faith and Eternal Hope for the Elusive American Dream

The Chinese often immigrated blindly to *Maiguo* — "may gwau," Chinese for "beautiful country," the name given to America in the last century — in search of the elusive American dream of prosperity, happiness, and a good life. Their parents and grandparents who left China, Taiwan, Hong Kong, and other Asian countries carry on this hope for their children and grandchildren, generations after the first Chinese immigrants encountered anti-Chinese sentiment.

Chinese immigrants, like their European American immigrant counterparts, came to America looking for a new and brighter be-

A young woman performs a traditional Chinese ribbon dance at a holiday celebration. Many folk customs such as this one are passed down from one generation to the next.

ginning. But unlike many immigrant groups, Chinese Americans still experience discrimination and feelings of being an outsider. As a result, today's generations of American-Born Chinese (called ABCs) often feel foreign in their own native land. So Chinese American parents hang onto their American dream by placing their hopes in their children's future. For many Chinese, the faith needed to keep this dream alive is as strong as — or stronger than — any religion.

Costumed performers portray an elder carrying a youth during a ceremonial dance. As the dance signifies, elders are expected to pass along traditional Chinese customs to younger generations.

CHAPTER FIVE

CUSTOMS, EXPRESSIONS, AND HOSPITALITY
NOURISHING THE SPIRIT

From private family birthday gatherings to wedding banquets and other large, elaborate community events, Chinese Americans express their hospitality and their many social customs in every celebration. With thousands of years of practice, Chinese food and health have become famous around the world. Keeping these cherished Chinese customs alive while adapting them to life in America has put Chinese Americans in the enviable position of having the best of both worlds.

Adopting American Social Customs

Michael and Sarah are looking forward to a summer vacation with their parents. They are joining their neighbors, the Martins, and their two children, Amy and Al, for a camping trip to Yellowstone National Park. Like other Americans, they enjoy the freedom to travel and explore the country and its different people and attractions.

The Lee family also shares in celebrating American historical events like the Fourth of July by watching local parades, marching with the school band, and joining family and friends for picnics and fireworks. Other honored American customs such as Labor Day weekend barbecues, Thanksgiving Day family feasts, and family reunions also contribute to their social life and are celebrated along with traditional Chinese holidays.

Like most American teenagers, Chinese American teens don blue jeans and the latest American fashions; hang out at shopping centers and drive-ins; listen to rock music, classic rock 'n' roll, pop, jazz, blues, and rap; and celebrate birthdays, graduations, weddings, and funerals just like their neighbors. Since the United States is a large country, Americans often base their style of clothing, music, and social customs on regional preferences in addition to religious, family, and personal ones.

The customs people adopt may be the ones that grandparents, mothers, fathers, aunts, uncles, and cousins share with family members. Because we all enjoy and need common experiences and stability in our lives, we adopt customs from family, friends, and community. Singing "Happy Birthday" is as natural to most Americans as making a wish and blowing out the candles on the cake. People carry out these customs without questioning why, because they have learned that by doing so, they share a common and meaningful way of celebrating.

Chinese American social customs may include both American and Chinese traditions, a natural blending of old and new, reflecting a family's dual heritage. For ex-

CHINESE CRISPY-SKIN CHICKEN

Here is a delicious way to prepare fried chicken, taken from a Chinese family recipe.

2 chickens (broiler fryers) (about 2 1/2 pounds) cut into serving-size pieces
   water

Honey and soy sauce marinade:
1/2 cup honey
1/4 cup vinegar
1 tablespoon molasses
1/2 cup soy sauce

Coating mixture:
3/4 cup sifted all-purpose flour
1 tablespoon salt
1 quart vegetable oil for deep frying

Wash and dry the chicken pieces. In a large skillet with a tight-fitting lid, place the chicken in two cups of water; bring to a boil. Reduce the heat; simmer, covered, for forty-five minutes, or until the chicken is tender.

Drain the chicken and rinse in cold water; dry well with paper towels.

While the chicken is drying, combine the honey, vinegar, molasses, soy sauce, and two tablespoons of water in a small bowl. Brush the chicken with this marinade and let it dry for about five minutes; then brush again with the same marinade.

Coat the chicken on all sides with the combined flour and salt coating mixture.

Slowly heat the vegetable oil in a deep fryer or in a deep, heavy kettle to 375° F on a deep-frying thermometer. Fry the chicken, a few pieces at a time, until golden brown, about two to three minutes. Drain the chicken on paper towels and serve at once.

Makes six servings.

ample, Chinese who live in China do not celebrate Thanksgiving, because it's an American holiday. But Chinese Americans do, joining their neighbors in celebrating the communal feast between American Indians and early immigrants from Europe. Chinese Americans follow the American custom of roasting a turkey for Thanksgiving, but some prepare it in a traditional Chinese style by basting the bird with a honey and soy sauce marinade. They stuff the turkey with scallions, Chinese black mushrooms, brown bean paste, and five-spice seasonings instead of American-style bread dressing. While the meaning of Thanksgiving remains the same, Chinese Americans keep customs from both cultures alive by creatively blending traditions that have evolved over the centuries.

The Nourishment of Life

Food has always held a central role in Chinese life. In China, food was not always abundant; even up through the mid-1950s, famines killing thousands of people were not uncommon in China. As a consequence, a good harvest became a time of great celebration. Family and village gatherings often coincided with these feasts. Eventually, it became a custom to always have a feast at family gatherings. This is especially true in the United States, a nation that immigrants from many places have often considered the "land of plenty."

The Family Table

Chinese Americans follow American meal customs, eating three meals daily with snacks in between. With their emphasis on family togetherness, Chinese

Americans try to share dinner with family members whenever possible. Children help set the table with a pair of chopsticks, a soup spoon, and a rice bowl for each setting. Traditional Chinese American dinners include a big bowl of soup placed in the middle of the table from which each family member eats using his or her own spoon. If guests are invited, the children add an individual soup bowl, a small serving plate, and a shallow dish for sauces at each place, along with the usual setting used for family dinners. As part of the evening dinner routine, children are asked to wash the rice in preparation for cooking it, much as children in other American households might be asked to make the salad for their family's meal.

Steamed rice customarily is served with all Chinese meals. The Chinese diet contains less red meat than a typical American meal. Pork, chicken, and seafood are commonly served with plenty of fresh vegetables. For the Chinese, eating more vegetables and less meat grew out of necessity in a land that did not support raising cattle for food. Traditional Chinese vegetables now found in many

A mother uses chopsticks to feed her younger daughter. Rice bowls and chopsticks are standard table settings in many Chinese American homes.

American supermarkets include bok choy, nappa (a variety of Chinese cabbage), Chinese parsley (also called cilantro), bean sprouts, long green beans, ginger, snow peas, bamboo shoots, and water chestnuts.

Newborn and Birthday Celebrations

Chinese culture looks at birthdays somewhat differently than Western culture. For example, old fashioned Chinese with ancient

BEAUTY AND THE BOWL

Most Americans have heard of reading tea leaves at the bottom of teacups to tell the fortune of the drinker, but Chinese mothers use the custom of reading rice at the bottom of a bowl to get their children to eat dinner. Chinese mothers tell their sons and daughters they can predict the beauty of a future marriage partner by how clean their rice bowls are at the end of a meal. The amount of food or rice left at the bottom of their rice bowls is said to foretell the condition of a future husband's or wife's complexion. The cleaner the bowl, the smoother the face; the dirtier the bowl, the rougher the face. Keep this in mind next time you have trouble finishing all the food on your plate.

by hardships of the land and time, and many infants did not survive their first month.

Today, Chinese Americans celebrate birthdays every year and count their age the same way other Americans do. But they also preserve the custom of celebrating a new birth. Great-grandmothers and grandmothers with traditional Chinese beliefs insist their granddaughters and daughters stay at home to rest for at least one month after giving birth, eating chicken soup and one poached egg every day, along with their other meals. In Chinese folklore, chicken represents the health and strength needed by the mom, and the egg signifies new life and fertility.

A bride wears a long Chinese silk gown at her wedding reception, changing from the American bridal gown worn at the church ceremony (see the picture on next page). Combining American and Chinese traditions is one way to express one's Chinese and American heritages.

Chinese traditions consider a baby already a year old at birth. They celebrate only two birthdays in a lifetime: one month after a newborn's birth and when he or she reaches sixty. In ancient times, Chinese peasants did not take for granted a newborn's health and survival. The average lifespan was shortened

At the end of the month, a banquet is held marking the newborn's birth, and family and friends gather for, of course, a feast. The new father's family passes out red-dyed boiled eggs to all the guests, as red symbolizes happy and festive times. It is a time to celebrate.

Wedding Banquets and Table Manners

A wedding provides another occasion to celebrate with family and friends by throwing a banquet. Which family pays for this usually large and expensive event depends on whose custom prevails. According to American custom, the bride's family hosts the dinner and reception. With old Confucian influences stressing a son's loyalty to family, Chinese custom expects the groom's family to celebrate the marriage with an elaborate banquet fit for emperors and empresses. Since food is so central to all social festivities, at least ten courses are expected at this gala occasion.

To make sure their guests are satisfied, hosts try to provide enough dinner courses to leave diners with no room to eat another bite. Guests are not considered impolite if they indulge heavily in eating and talking at a wedding banquet. However, it would be rude to not eat enough rice, or to touch food from a common bowl of food without taking any from it.

The modern Chinese American bride may choose to blend Chinese and American customs in food or fashion. Traditional Chinese brides wear a long silk brocade gown, usually red with a phoenix and a dragon embroidered on the front. Today, a Chinese American bride may wear this *cheong som* (pronounced "churn som" in Cantonese, meaning "long gown") at her rehearsal dinner or at the wedding reception and a traditional American white bridal gown for the church ceremony.

Another Chinese custom often adopted by Chinese American couples is the method of signing in their guests. Instead of asking friends and family to sign in with a pen on the pages of a bound guest book, Chinese tradition calls for the use of a large square piece of red silk and ink-filled fountain pens. Guests sign their names and greeting in Chinese

Following the ceremony, the bride and groom show off the silk "guest book," a square red piece of cloth often decorated with elaborate embroidery on which guests sign in.

characters (English is acceptable, of course!), creating a personalized keepsake that can be displayed in the newlyweds' home.

Funerals

When a member of a Chinese American community dies, family and friends gather to offer support to the loved ones in much the same way other Americans do. A funeral ceremony is held at the burial site, followed by a meal at the family's home. The family serves an abundance of meat dishes to honor

Funeral florals are placed on and inside a car in preparation for a street procession enroute to the burial site.

the deceased, and traditional Buddhists believe these dishes also satisfy any hungry ancestral ghosts who may be present.

In some largely first-generation Chinese communities, mourners walk in street processions, complete with mourning musicians, from the temple in Chinatown to the burial site, if it is nearby. Chinese Americans who have adopted more Western customs drive a procession of cars to the burial site, in the tradition of American funerals.

Dim Sum and Chinese Tea Houses

One of the best-known social customs passed to generations of Chinese Americans is *dim sum* (meaning "to touch the heart"), a time-honored Chinese tradition from Hong Kong and the Guangdong, or Canton, Province in southern China. Family, friends, or business associates get together for tea and delicious Chinese snacks, usually sometime between late morning and mid-afternoon on a Saturday or Sunday.

Dim sum is served at Chinese tea houses, most of them in Chinatowns. The pace is leisurely, the atmosphere noisy and informal. Talking loudly above the clatter of plates, cups, and tea carts banging against tables and chairs, visitors take time to sample a little bit from a variety of Chinese delights. Tea house guests find lots of Chinese snacks to choose from: meat and seafood filling wrapped in a thin pastry, steamed and fried; shrimp balls; sweet rolls and tarts; noodles; soups; and baked meat-filled sweet buns. It's no wonder this popular Chinese custom is enjoyed by Chinese Americans as well as others.

Food and Medicine

"You are what you eat." We often hear these words when people discuss diet. The Chinese consider food and medicine to be the same, not making the distinctions between them that most Americans make. The Chinese also see no difference between what Americans call "health foods" and other foods in the Chinese diet.

The Healing Properties of Hot and Cold Foods. Since Confucian times, the Chinese have understood the role of food in promoting good health and avoiding disease. Today, Chinese Americans as well as other Americans practice healthy Chinese cooking styles, selecting the freshest ingredients and preparing well-balanced, tasty recipes.

Foods contain different properties, which can be described as hot (*yang*) or cold (*yin*). Eating the right foods can keep you healthy or heal minor ailments. For example, fresh ginger contains yang, or hot properties, which are perfect for fighting off stomach aches and diarrhea caused by yin, or cold properties. Drinking too much of a cold beverage, such as soda or a milk shake, can make you sick to your stomach if you don't counterbalance the yin with yang, or hot foods. A Chinese remedy would be a hot and sour soup with some fresh ginger in the recipe. Traditional Chinese mothers would not suggest drinking a tall glass of cold milk after eating a healing bowl of hot and sour soup, believing that any benefit of the hot yang soup would be offset by the cold yin milk.

"Eat this . . . it's good for you." American kids have heard these words more times than they can — or care to — remember. For many Americans, however, these words are a source of eating pleasure, since they can be said about most Chinese food. And as we'll see in the next chapter, eating Chinese food is not only "good for you," but when it's shared around the table and served with chopsticks, bowls of steaming rice, and tea, it's also a lot of fun — and entirely American.

A GREAT GIFT IDEA: AMERICAN-GROWN GINSENG

Ginseng is as integral to Asian cultures as hot dogs and apple pie are to American culture.

The Chinese revere the nutritional powers of ginseng, an aromatic root grown in parts of China and the United States. From early times, those who used this root in ancient recipes have claimed that ginseng has a general strengthening effect, as well as raising physical and mental capacity for work. Ginseng also is said to lower stress in those who consume it.

Ironically, the best ginseng in the world is grown not in China but in the United States. Ginsenoside, the natural ingredient found in ginseng, gives the root its anti-stress benefits. Researchers from the Ginseng Board of Wisconsin and the Ginseng Research Institute of America have found that American-grown ginseng contains higher levels of ginsenoside than Korean and Chinese White ginseng.

Considered superior in quality to Chinese crops, North American-grown ginseng makes a very desirable gift for the Chinese from Americans and Chinese Americans living here. Top North American ginseng farmers are located in Wausau, Wisconsin, as well as in northern California and Vancouver, British Columbia. Conditions in Wisconsin are especially ideal for cultivating ginseng, making the state one of the largest exporters of American-grown ginseng to the markets of Hong Kong and Taiwan.

The beauty of Tai Chi Chuan, a Chinese martial arts form, is demonstrated at a public park. Highlighted by the World Trade Center, the New York City skyline looms in the distance.

CONTRIBUTIONS TO AMERICAN CULTURE
AS AMERICAN AS CHOP SUEY

"Let's have Chinese tonight!": What a welcome and familiar suggestion in many American homes today. Busy lifestyles and a fascination with new and different tastes from around the world have created a permanent place for Chinese food in America. What began as a periodic "chop suey" takeout and fortune cookie has now grown to a sometimes weekly habit of ordering out, or going out, for Chinese food. Most European immigrants in the late 1800s did not easily adopt the tradi-

tional recipes and foods brought over by Chinese immigrants. But innovative Chinese chefs adapted authentic recipes from their homeland to cater to customers who were used to a different diet. Today, mainstream America has adopted many customs and traditions from the many ethnic heritages represented by its citizens. Included among these are authentic Chinese traditions as well as American adaptations of Chinese culture.

The owner of a Chinese restaurant serves dinner to her customers. Both authentic Chinese food and American dishes like chop suey are prepared for Chinese and non-Chinese patrons alike.

Mandarin pancakes, a kind of Chinese bread, are prepared in this Chinese restaurant. These are usually served to complement soups and rice *congee*, a regular part of a traditional Chinese diet.

Chinese Culture Embedded in Mainstream America

Cuisine. Meals in China usually consist of bigger portions of vegetables, rice, or noodles, and a small amount of fish or poultry. Since pork and beef are usually in short supply, these are reserved for special holiday and other festival banquets. An American adaptation of authentic Chinese recipes is "chop suey," a mixture mostly made up of meat and gravy, with a few vegetables, served over a small serving of steamed rice. Chinese living in China do not know what chop suey is, since it is a recipe invented by a Chinese chef for his non-Chinese customers.

As more and more Americans from all national backgrounds opened up their minds and pocketbooks to experience different cultures, Chinese businesses looked for ways to attract a growing trade, tourism. Rather than cakes, pies, or pastries, traditional Chinese menus feature oranges and other fresh fruit to top off dinner, so Chinese restaurateurs in San Francisco invented the fortune cookie to satisfy the sweet tooth of tourists in Chinatown.

Mainstream American culture includes many things that are Chinese or of Chinese origin, extending beyond takeout food. American taste for authentic Chinese cuisine has grown in the past decade as internationally grown ingredients have become easier to buy, making dishes like kung pao chicken, moo shu pork, and sweet and sour shrimp as familiar as the variety of Italian pastas available to satisfy American appetites.

Art, Architecture, and Design. From commercial buildings and city streetscaping to home living rooms and outdoor gardens, Chinese art and culture have influenced the way Americans design their buildings and reshape the landscape. I. M. Pei, an award-winning and widely respected architect, has helped lay a sound foundation to city infrastructures in America and around the world. Frank Lloyd Wright, one of the twentieth century's best-known American architects, gained creative insight through his travels to Asian and European countries. Wright designed buildings and gardens that strongly reflect the simplicity and elegance of Chinese art and design. The Ginko tree, with its hardy characteristics and origins outside a monastery in China, has been widely used by city planners and architects for streetscaping, especially in the Midwest.

Inside many American homes, Oriental rugs, porcelain, chinaware, and paintings can be found with definite Chinese influences. For example, blue and white willow patterns became popular for vases and chinaware when the British and other Europeans began trade with China. Recognizing China as a major marketplace, international traders eventually brought silks, copper, paper, gunpowder, and, of course, Chinese food and spices into American homes. Remember the long history of contributions that the Chinese have made to American lives today as you pull out a piece of paper to do your homework or go out to fly a kite. In addition to inventing paper, the Chinese thought of unique ways to have fun with it. Paper folding to form toys and other objects (also known by the Japanese name, *origami*) originated in China, as did kitemaking.

American architect Ieoh Ming (I. M.) Pei poses with the frame of his glass pyramid at the Palais du Louvre in Paris, France, in 1985. Pei's designs may be found throughout the U.S. and abroad.

FRUITFUL CONTRIBUTIONS

Chinese immigrants rightfully deserve credit for some significant innovations and contributions to American agriculture. For example, the bing cherry was a hybrid fruit developed by a Chinese fruit grower named Ah Bing in the 1870s in Oregon. In the 1880s, Lue Gim Gong began experimenting in Massachusetts with different varieties of apples, currants, peaches, grapefruit, tomatoes, and raspberries. He is best known for the variety of orange that bears his name (Gim, pronounced "gum" in Cantonese, the Chinese name for tangerines) and for which he won the Wilder Medal for the U.S. Department of Agriculture in 1911.

Building A Nation

The first Chinese immigrants to America in the mid-1800s were mostly poor and uneducated. But their optimism and desire to improve their station in life gave them the incentive to work hard. Their contributions were measured in the miles of railroad track laid and the cities and towns that grew up along those same routes.

While building the railroad was a significant contribution, Chinese hard work, skills, and dedication furthered the growth, development and industrialization of the United States in many other ways as well. For example, Chinese were instrumental in the development of agriculture in the western states, serving as migrant farm workers and sharecroppers.

Bringing their knowledge of irrigation and agronomy with them from China, they helped turn dry central California into pro-

INTERNATIONAL RECOGNITION FOR ACHIEVEMENTS

Chinese American scientists Tsung Dao Lee (shown at right) and Chen Ning Yang together won the Nobel Prize for Physics in 1957. In 1976, another Chinese American physicist, Samuel Ting, won the same prize. And scientist Chien-Shiun Wu, who was instrumental in proving the Yang-Lee theory which led to their winning the Nobel Prize in 1957, herself was honored with the Cyrus B. Comstock Award of the National Academy of Sciences for her discoveries in the field of electricity, magnetism, and radiation.

In the field of architecture, I.M. (Ieoh Ming) Pei, the famous architect who designed the East Wing of the National Gallery of Art in Washington, won the Gold Medal of the American Institute of Architecture in 1979.

ductive farmland. They were fisherman and tradesmen. They were skilled artisans and craftsmen. They worked in factories and mills throughout the United States. And as the U.S. economy evolved, so did the manner in which Asians contributed.

Today, in a different way, the descendants of these Chinese pioneers also strive to contribute and be successful. In 1943, the repeal of the Chinese Exclusion Act finally allowed additional Chinese to join those who had immigrated before 1882. Many of the newer wave of Chinese immigrants were educated, emigrating to America to attend universities as well as to take jobs as doctors, engineers, scientists, and business people. Today, Chinese Americans participate in nearly every walk of life in America, making valuable contributions to the activities in which they are involved.

The Confucian tradition brought to America by the first immigrants taught them to value education as the way to better oneself and improve one's life. After the founding of the People's Republic of China in 1949, thousands of Chinese students came to the U.S. to earn college undergraduate and graduate degrees. Many of them would one day return to China to help provide direction and expertise to a young nation. Still others would stay in the U.S. and become productive, educated members of American society.

As a result of their hard work, the Chinese have become stereotyped by their chosen occupations. Many see Chinese Americans in terms of their historical experience: an industrious, dedicated group, yet largely passive, striving to fit in and become part of the U.S. mainstream. Later generations of Chinese Americans are breaking these previous

Chinese American newswoman Connie Chung joined Dan Rather as CBS co-anchor in May 1993. Chung has become one of the most prominent Asian American women on a major TV network.

Communicating Positive Values

Perhaps the most powerful way to communicate ideas in our society is through the most common sources of information, such as television, radio, movies, books, newspapers, magazines, and advertising. These forms of communication reach large numbers of people and can communicate an image or idea over and over, making it stick in people's minds.

TV and newspapers have provided a source of income and professional advancement for Chinese Americans; they have also given Chinese Americans a chance to break down many of the negative images that had once been promoted by TV, the movies, and the press. In broadcast journalism, for example, Chinese Americans have long held jobs producing news programs but have

Charlie Chan, an exaggerated Hollywood creation, is portrayed in this 1937 movie still by Warner Oland, a non-Chinese actor (right). Also shown: Asian American actor Keye Luke.

seldom been seen in the limelight. Slowly, this is changing. Connie Chung is a broadcast journalist and news anchor for a major television network. At the local level, Linda Wu is a broadcast journalist and anchor for a major television station in Chicago. Debra Wong covered the Persian Gulf War in 1990 for National Public Radio and became famous for her reporting. Although discrimination still exists, Chinese Americans have made great strides toward overcoming historical stereotypes and professional limitations.

stereotypes by seeking individual achievement and recognition in a wide variety of roles. Since the end of World War II, many Chinese Americans have entered professional life in medicine, engineering, architecture, law, publishing, and many other occupations once considered off limits to foreigners.

Another powerful medium for creating and furthering both negative and positive images is film, and for many years Hollywood played a powerful role in keeping Chinese Americans out of the social mainstream.

Traditional Chinese custom dictates that the Chinese act with deference for elders, behave in a reserved manner, respond politely, and speak softly, not provoking others with their words or tone of voice. For the Chinese, these were positive traits. Other Americans, however, didn't understand the reasons for Chinese reserve.

In the early days of moviemaking, Hollywood reinforced popular stereotypes of Chinese as docile, passive, mysterious, and, sometimes, evil. The "inscrutable Chinaman" was a common character in such movies as *The Yellow Peril* (1908), *Dr. Foo* (1914), and *The Mysterious Dr. Fu Manchu* (1929).

Even when Hollywood tried to be more generous to the Chinese, the movie industry often simply created a different stereotype, one that moviemakers believed to be more positive. Instead of talking like real people, characters in these movies dispensed "fortune-cookie wisdom," which oversimplified or denigrated Chinese traditions and customs. The famous Charlie Chan character is an example of such treatment: The

Bruce Lee, the first Asian American film star to capture international attention, is shown here in his 1972 movie *Fists of Fury.* Since his death, Lee's legend as an expert martial artist and positive role model remains alive.

detective Chan, while always victorious in the end, was never seen as an equal with his peers.

More recently, a different stereotype was born with the rise of martial arts movies. Unlike many of the earlier movie images of Chinese and other Asians, however, the images of Asians in these movies have also led to the furthering of positive values for all Americans.

Most Americans know of Bruce Lee, the Chinese pop film star who introduced martial arts to mainstream American culture. Unfortunately, many Americans associated only the violent forms of martial arts with the Chinese and other Asian cultures, ignoring its positive traits. While most people saw Lee as a stereotyped, Gung Fu (pronounced "Kung Fu") action hero, he was also a devoted father and husband. Among the central themes in many Bruce Lee films were the defense of the weak, protection of family values, and respect for one's elders.

As one of the first Asian pop film stars to be accepted by Americans and Europeans, Bruce Lee became one of the first positive role models for Chinese Americans. Today, many parents send their children to karate or judo classes to promote such positive traits as self-discipline, physical skill, and self-confidence.

Portraying a Truer Image of Women

For many years, films portrayed stereotypical Asian women as ultra-feminine, enigmatic, mysterious creatures, incapable of independent thought and totally reliant for their salvation on a man, usually a man of European background. Famous movies such as *The World of Suzy Wong* and *Flower Drum Song* are typical of this sort of rendition.

Fortunately, today's modern Chinese American women have done much to dispel these early stereotypes. Many have matched accomplishments of other American men and women in business, education, government, and medicine. And as Chinese American women begin to make their mark in the arts

and film industry, they use the opportunity to change the way Asian women are portrayed. In the movie *The Joy Luck Club,* based on the best-selling novel by Chinese American Amy Tan, true-to-life Chinese American women are shown in their diversity of intelligence, sensitivity, wit, and humor. Tan teamed up with another Chinese American, Wayne Wang, an accomplished film producer, to make this movie one that reached across cultural boundaries to touch Americans from different ethnic backgrounds and bring credit to women of all groups and generations.

The Written Word

When it comes to communicating Chinese culture and traditions to mainstream America, Chinese American authors have had relatively more success with the written word than on the big screen. Starting as early as 1909, Chinese American authors have been writing about their experiences in the United States. One of the themes of this literature has been the accurate depiction of the Chinese and their experiences.

My Life in China and *America,* by Wing Yung (1909), and J. S. Tow's *The Real Chinese in America* (1923) were among the first attempts to tell a balanced story of Chinese American life. Later on, books such as *Father and Glorious Descendant* (1943), by Pardee Lowe, explored the difficulties of maintaining links to two different cultures, Chinese and American.

But these works and others by Chinese authors focused only on the positive aspects of being Chinese in America, rather than telling the full story. It was not until the Asian American Pride movement in the 1960s that Chinese American authors broke the tradition of merely explaining their culture and began portraying the entire experience, hardships as well as successes, of being Chinese American. Louis Chu's *Eat a Bowl of Tea* (1961) described the hard life in New York City's Chinatown during the Exclusion Act in gritty, honest terms never before used to describe Chinese Americans. In the 1970s, other authors such as Amy Tan (*The Joy Luck Club*) and Maxine Hong Kingston (*China Men*) found a wider audience in mainstream America for their stories of culture and social history.

Making Their Voices Heard

Chinese Americans have traditionally been known for quietly "blending in" with mainstream American culture. Having found, first in China and later in America, that attention often brought suffering and discrimination, the Chinese learned to blend into society and avoid notice.

Lacking command of the English language, many Chinese immigrants opted to hide in the background, toiling long hours in silence to earn a living and save enough to send back to their families in the old country. But silence is not always golden, as many cultural groups in America have learned. By the early 1960s, as the descendants of the first Chinese immigrant pioneers became more mainstream, they started to change the perception of Chinese Americans.

Critically acclaimed author Amy Tan relaxes during an interview for the opening of *The Joy Luck Club*, the movie based on her first and best-selling novel about four Chinese mothers and their migration to America.

The Civil Rights movement in the 1950s and 1960s was a widely recognized result of African Americans standing up for their rights. In a less vocal way, Chinese Americans also spoke out to secure their civil liberties. Many Chinese Americans could identify with the philosophy of Dr. Martin Luther King.

CHINESE AMERICAN MEN AND WOMEN: BREAKING NEW GROUND

One of the most controversial yet meaningful accomplishments by a Chinese American came with the selection of a design by Yale University architecture student Maya Lin (shown below) for the Vietnam War Memorial in Washington, D.C. With its streamlined, minimalist "V" design, "The Wall" is viewed daily by thousands of visitors who are touched by the emotional impact of its stark design and the power of its symbolism.

In another groundbreaking achievement, Michael Chang (shown at right), at the age of seventeen, won the 1989 French Open Tennis Tournament, becoming both the youngest man to ever win a Grand Slam title and the first American to win top honors in that French tournament since 1955.

Numerous organizations born in the Civil Rights era focused on aiding Asians in their quest for equal treatment. In New York City, the Chinatown Planning Council was established to help develop the local Chinese community. Other organizations provided social services and relief efforts not available from government agencies. Several of the larger Chinatown communities set up legal service offices to help the Chinese when they had legal problems and to represent the community in matters involving civil and legal rights. The Asian Americans for Equal Employment (AAFEE) organization was created to help protect the rights of Asian workers.

Today, organizations such as the Organization of Chinese Americans, Inc., (OCA) speak on behalf of the more than 1.6 million citizens and residents of Chinese ancestry in America. They fight for social justice, equal opportunity, and equal treatment, while working to eliminate prejudice and ignorance by sharing the cultural heritage of Chinese and other Asian Americans with the rest of our society.

Bringing A Healthy Balance

Like their relatives in China, many Chinese Americans enjoy such popular sports as basketball, volleyball, and tennis. But the Chinese have contributed more than just their love for major American sports to the world of health and recreation.

In food and exercise, Chinese immigrants have brought to America an ancient tradition

A volleyball tournament takes place at a Chinatown playground. Many Chinese here and abroad have enjoyed this popular sport for years.

of healthy balance and harmony, making the most of natural resources from the land as well as the mind, soul, and body. In a society that seems to be searching endlessly for eternal youth and fitness, the Chinese martial arts and focus on healthy eating have become a permanent — and genuinely healthful — part of life for many.

Tai Chi Chuan is an ancient martial art and exercise, extremely popular both in China and among Asians in the U.S. It is a relaxing

Two martial arts instructors take a break between classes. Many Americans participate in Tai Chi Chuan and other martial art forms for sports, recreation, and self-defense.

activity, designed to exercise every part of the body and bring the entire body and soul into harmony with the world and its forces. Other martial arts also popular in the U.S. include Taekwondo (a Korean martial art) and Aikido (a Japanese martial art popularized by the American actor Stephen Seagal). While nearly all of the martial arts have their roots in the military or self-defense, today they are more often seen as sport and recreation for the American mainstream.

Food and Health

Food is one of the glories of Chinese civilization and one of China's important contributions to world culture. Its rich culinary tradition survives today outside China's great dynasties, in cities and towns throughout America. A famous Cantonese saying

about Guangdong (Canton), "Every five steps a restaurant," is true of most Chinatowns in America, where Asians and non-Asians alike sample authentic Chinese cooking and culture. And where there are no Chinatowns, Chinese restaurants and take-outs are still a mainstay of American life.

With the increase of trade with China and the growing American fondness for international cuisine, Americans can find most of the ingredients needed to prepare Chinese recipes at home in their local supermarkets. Contributing to the rise of Chinese cooking at home is the popularity of such cooking utensils as the wok, a stir-fry pan requiring little oil for healthful cooking. Chinese cooking styles also form the base of other cuisines — Japanese, Vietnamese, and Thai — that enjoy popularity at restaurants across America.

Leaders in Business, Education, and Government

Many Chinese Americans have risen to fame and success in the fields of business, education, and government. An Wang made Wang Computers a world leader in mini-computer-based word processing and general computing. Gerald Tsai, Jr., became the chief executive officer of the American Can Company, a long-established U.S. business, in 1986.

In education and science, Dr. Chang-lin Tien was named the chancellor of the University of California at Berkeley, one of the nation's most prestigious institutions of higher learning. In 1991, Stanley ManFung Yuen received the Eta Kappa Nu Recognition Award as the nation's most outstanding electrical engineer under the age of thirty-six. And Dr. Taylor Wong, a Chinese American physicist, became the second Asian American to fly in space when he flew aboard the *Challenger* space shuttle in May 1985.

Throughout the United States, many Chinese Americans hold elected or appointed government offices. S. B. Woo was elected to be the lieutenant governor of the state of Delaware. Michael Woo, a Los Angeles city councilman, ran unsuccessfully for mayor of Los Angeles in 1993. And Cheryl Lau was elected to be the State Treasurer of Nevada.

Quite a few Chinese Americans have been appointed to judgeships as well, includ-

Michael Woo, 1993 Los Angeles mayoral candidate, was endorsed by President Bill Clinton. Woo fought a close race against his millionaire opponent and raised the status of Asian Americans in the national political arena.

ing William Richardson and Herman Lum, both chief justices on the Hawaii Supreme Court. Thomas Tang sits on the U.S. Ninth Circuit Court of Appeals in Arizona.

These are just a handful of the many Chinese and other Asian Americans who are contributing to American society today. Slowly, and with dogged determination, Chinese Americans are making their presence known and appreciated.

CHRONOLOGY

5000 B.C. Archaeologists' date for signs of civilization in what is today the People's Republic of China.

551-479 B.C. The period in which Confucius, one of the most influential Chinese philosophers, lived.

A.D. 499 A priest named Hui Shen reportedly arrives in what is today called America.

1830 The first census to document Chinese in America records three Chinese in all of the U.S.; subsequent census counts for the Chinese rise to eight in 1840 and 748 in 1850.

1848 The discovery of gold in California sets off a large wave of immigration from China; by 1852, Chinese immigration to America increases to twenty-five thousand.

1854 Local Chinese elders form the Chinese Six Companies to protect and run U.S. Chinese communities.

1856 Foreign miners are taxed in order to prevent the Chinese from panning for gold.

1859 Chinese students are excluded from attending public schools in San Francisco.

1860 Two companies are contracted to build the first transcontinental railroad in America.

1863 Recruiting begins in China to bring laborers to work on the Central Pacific Railroad.

1864 The U.S. Civil War creates a serious labor shortage.

1868 The Sino-American Treaty is signed, allowing Chinese immigration for "purposes of curiosity, trade, or permanent residence" but restricting the right of Chinese to become naturalized U.S. citizens.

1869 May 10: the "Golden Spike" celebration at Promontory Point, Utah, marks the joining of the two ends of the transcontinental railroad; though Chinese workers contributed as much as 90 percent of the labor used to complete the railroad, they are not officially recognized at this ceremony.

1870 The Naturalization Act excludes the Chinese from becoming U.S. citizens and prohibits wives of Chinese laborers from entering the U.S.

1870-1879 The Chinese become scapegoats during the U.S. recession; as the economy collapses, rioting mobs destroy many Chinese communities in California and other West Coast states.

1870 Chinese fruit grower Ah Bing develops the cherry that bears his name.

1882 The Chinese Exclusion Act is passed, keeping families from joining immigrants already in America.

1892 The Geary Act is passed, prohibiting Chinese immigration for another ten years.

1902 Congress indefinitely extends the Chinese Exclusion Act, prohibiting the Chinese from immigration.

1906 San Francisco Chinese, Korean, and Japanese children are sent to the segregated Oriental Public School.

1910-1940 Angel Island, in San Francisco Bay, is set up as a detention center for the non-laboring class of Chinese immigrants; the Chinese and other Asian immigrants are separated from their families and undergo grueling examinations before given entry to the U.S.; some are detained in the prisonlike barracks for as long as two years, and many, unable to tolerate the inhumane conditions, commit suicide.

1920s Chinatowns sprout up in North American cities with large Chinese populations.

1921 A special act directed against Chinese women prevents them from automatically becoming U.S. citizens upon marrying American citizens.

1924 A second Exclusion Act prevents immigration for Chinese who do not have at least a master's degree.

1930s America's Great Depression sets off riots and attacks against the Chinese and other Asians.

1932 The Cable Act is passed, decreeing that U.S.-born Chinese American women marrying foreign-born Asians automatically lose their citizenship.

1943	The Chinese Exclusion Act passed in 1882 is finally repealed with the Magnuson Act, ending the exclusion of Chinese entry to America over a sixty-year period.
1952	The Immigration and Nationality Act is passed, granting the rights of naturalization and eventual citizenship for foreign-born Asians with a quota of 105 immigrants per year for each Asian country.
1957	Nobel Prizes in Physics are awarded to Chinese Americans Dr. Chen-ning Yang and Dr. Tsung-dao Lee.
1965	Discriminatory immigration laws end, opening up U.S. immigration to Asian countries.
1966	Chinese American Gerald Tsai starts up the Manhattan Fund as the "go go" years begin on Wall Street.
1976	Chinese American Samuel Ting wins the Nobel Prize for Physics.
1979	I. M. (Ieoh Ming) Pei, the architect who is designing the Guest Wing of the National Gallery of Art in Washington, D.C., wins the Gold Medal of the American Institute of Architecture; architectural student Maya Lin submits the winning design for the Vietnam War Memorial in Washington, D.C.
1981	Congress grants Taiwan a separate immigration quota, helping to reunite families.
1983	Chinese American Vincent Chin is beaten to death with a baseball bat by two men in Detroit, Michigan; rather than receiving prison sentences, the men are given probation, causing Chinese American and Asian outrage throughout the U.S.; eventually, one of the men is found guilty and sentenced to twenty-five years in prison for violating Vincent Chin's civil rights.
1985	May 1: Dr. Taylor Wong, physicist, becomes the first Chinese American in space when he flies aboard the *Challenger* space shuttle.
1989	Michael Chang, at the age of seventeen, wins the French Open Tennis Tournament, becoming the first American to win top honors in that event since 1955.
1990	Dr. Chang-lin Tien is named chancellor of the University of California at Berkeley, one of the nation's most prestigious institutions of higher learning.
1991	Engineer Stanley Man Fung Yuen receives the Eta Kappa Nu Recognition Award as the nation's most outstanding electrical engineer under the age of thirty-six.

GLOSSARY

Bachelor Societies	Groups formed in America by Chinese men in the absence of Chinese women, who were not allowed to emigrate to the U.S. in large numbers until after World War II.
Buddhism	One of three major ancient religions in China; Buddhism began in India and spread to Southeast Asia, where it was adopted by the Chinese several hundred years before the birth of Christ.
Calligraphy	An art form that presents written characters as central themes or ideas. Chinese writing, in which each character represents an idea or a word, is sometimes called calligraphy.
Cantonese	A spoken Chinese dialect of southern China.
Chinatown	A community of Chinese people, residences, and businesses, usually in an urban setting formed in the 1920s and 1930s as a way to create a comfortable environment where native Chinese customs, languages, and food could be shared without criticism.
Chinese Six Companies	A specific group of *tongs,* or associations of families, established by Chinese migrants to run their society in California around the time of the 1849 California gold rush.

Confucianism	One of the three major ancient religions or systems of thought in China.
Dim sum	A morning to mid-afternoon meal made up of a wide variety of meat- and vegetable-filled dumplings, cakes, or buns served in Chinese tea houses and restaurants. *Dim sum* means "a little bit of heart" in Chinese.
Discrimination	Treating a person or group differently based merely on perceived differences in background.
Eurasian	A person, group, or culture blending European and Asian heritages.
Exclusion Act	A law passed by the U.S. Congress to limit immigration from certain countries.
Extended family	Aunts, uncles, cousins, and even unrelated members of the Chinese and non-Chinese community who are considered important to the immediate family.
Ginseng	An herbal root thought to have medicinal properties and highly valued by the Chinese.
Lunar New Year	The part of the Chinese astrological calendar that marks the beginning of the new year, usually between late January and early February on the Western (Gregorian) calendar.
Mandarin	A spoken dialect of northern China. A version of it has become China's national language.
Model Minority Myth	A stereotype that depicts all Asians as well-educated, hard-working, disciplined, and non-threatening to the dominant group in America.
Naturalization	The legal process whereby immigrants receive citizenship from their adopted country.
Oriental	An old and outdated term used to label all Asian people. Oriental is correctly used to describe objects (such as art, carpets, vases, food) rather than people.
Philosophy	A system of beliefs used as a guide to living.
Scapegoat	An entity, group, or person wrongfully blamed, especially during difficult times.
Tai Chi Chuan	An ancient martial art form.
Taoism	One of the three major religions of China.
Tong	A family association based on surnames or place of geographic origin.
Wok	A stir-fry cooking vessel; the central utensil in just about every kitchen in China.

FURTHER READING

Clayre, Alasdair. *The Heart of the Dragon.* Boston: Houghton Mifflin Company, 1985.

Lim, S., M. Tsutakawa, and M. Donnelly, eds. *The Forbidden Stitch: An Asian American Women's Anthology.* Corvallis, Oreg.: Calyx Books, 1988.

McLenighan, Valgean. *China — A History to 1949.* Chicago: Childrens Press, 1983.

Meltzer, Milton. *The Chinese-Americans.* New York: Crowell, 1980.

Shui, Amy. *Chinese Food and Drink.* New York: Bookwright Press, 1987.

Terzi, Marinella. *The Chinese Empire.* Chicago: Childrens Press, 1992.

Wu, Dana Y. *The Chinese American Experience.* Brookfield, Conn.: Millbrook Press, 1993.

Yee, Paul. *Tales from Gold Mountain: Stories of the Chinese in the New World.* New York: Macmillan, 1989.

Yep, Laurence. *Mountain Light.* New York: Harper and Row, 1985.

Yep, Laurence. *Tongues of Jade.* New York: HarperCollins, 1991.

Yung, Judy. *Chinese Women of America: A Pictorial History.* Seattle: University of Washington Press, 1986.

INDEX